PICKLED & PACKED

PICKLED & PACKED

Recipes for artisanal pickles, preserves, relishes & cordials

Valerie AIKMAN-SMITH

PHOTOGRAPHY BY *Erin* KUNKEL

RYLAND PETERS & SMALL

LONDON • NEW YORK

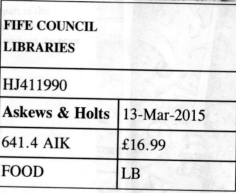

Designer Geoff Borin
Commissioning Editor Stephanie Milner
Production Manager Gordana Simakovic
Art Director Leslie Harrington
Editorial Director Julia Charles

Food Stylist Valerie Aikman-Smith
Prop Stylist Jennifer Barguiarena
Indexer Hilary Bird

First published in 2014 by Ryland Peters & Small,
20–21 Jockey's Fields, London WC1R 4BW
and
519 Broadway, 5th Floor, New York, NY 10012

www.rylandpeters.com

10 9 8 7 6 5 4 3 2 1

Text © Valerie Aikman-Smith 2014

Design and photographs © Ryland Peters & Small 2014

ISBN: 978-1-84975-490-3

A CIP record for this book is available from the British Library.

US Library of Congress CIP data has been applied for.

Printed in China

Food Safety Notice:

The information contained within this book is intended as a general guide to
preserving at home based on the author's recipe development and experience.
Although all reasonable care has been taken in the preparation of this book, neither
the publishers nor the author can accept any liability for any consequence from the
use thereof, or the information contained therein. Please consult an up-to-date
government source on food safety for further information.

Notes:

• All spoon measurements are level unless otherwise specified.

• All eggs are organic large (UK) or extra large (US), unless otherwise specified.

• Ovens should be preheated to the specified temperatures. We recommend using an
oven thermometer. If using a fan-assisted oven, adjust temperatures according to the
manufacturer's instructions.

• Weights and measurements have been rounded up or down slightly to make
measuring easier.

• When a recipe calls for the grated zest of lemons or limes or uses slices of fruit, buy
unwaxed fruit and wash well before using. If you can only find treated fruit, scrub well
in warm soapy water before using.

Contents

PRESERVING *techniques*

Preserving fruits and vegetables over the centuries has resulted in many techniques and recipes, from pickles, vinegars, relishes, mustards, candied fruit, and pastes, to bottling, liqueurs, and cordials.

Preserving food was necessary before refrigeration to make the most of the harvest and keep food for the long winter months. Of course now we have refrigerators but what could be better than reaching into your pantry and grabbing a wonderful jar of fruit or vegetables canned at the height of their season. So much better than buying out of season produce that has probably traveled half way around the world. We are lucky to have access to so many herbs, spices, and flavored vinegars to make the most interesting and delicious preserves. If you live in a large city you can shop easily for seasonal produce at farmers' markets. Or if you have a garden with a vegetable patch or are part of a community garden you could use your own fresh produce too.

Pickles always taste great with an acidic kick and gentle sweetness, and pickling is a very forgiving form of preserving so don't be afraid to invent new combinations of herbs and spices. In order for vinegar to act as an effective pickling liquor it should have at least 5 percent acetic acid content. A good tip is to roast mustard seeds and other spices that you are using in a hot pan for a couple of minutes to bring out the oils and aromatic flavors, making for a richer brine. Vinegars are the simplest of all preserves to make at home. Simply mix fruit, herbs, and spices together to create interesting flavors. Try to leave the herbs, fruit, or vegetables marinating in the vinegar for as long as you can as this will make for a deeper and more intense flavor. Fresh herbs such as tarragon, rosemary, thyme, and sage and robust fruits such as raspberries and blackberries work particularly well. My favorite discovery is the fantastic rose-scented vinegar produced when pickling rose petals (page 29).

Relishes and mustards are simple to make and keep especially well in the refrigerator. I like to store them in small, sterilized glass jars and have several open at the same time. Texan Hot Sauce (page 44) and Southern Mustard (page 63) are always good to have to hand.

Spoon fruits, candies, and pastes require a lot of sugar to preserve. I like to add strong herbs like rosemary and thyme to give an earthy taste, which complement sweet preserves. Roll candied peel (page 116) in flavored sugars such as lavender or maple to garnish dishes that use your homemade preserves.

Bottling fruit in a sugar syrup is the traditional method but you can change it up by using hearty bourbons, whiskies, and port to preserve prunes, cherries, and plums. Now you have delicious tipsy fruit and the bonus is the fruits have flavored the alcohol, which makes a great addition to any cocktail. Adding whole cinnamon sticks, bay leaves, curry leaves, and citrus leaves to bottled fruits and vegetables makes them look especially pretty while flavoring the contents of the jars.

Delicious lip-smacking drinks can also be made with sharp sweet orange bitters (page 125), stone fruit liqueurs (page 135) and homemade cordials (pages 134–140) so become a mixologist and start by making your own. Cordials are the perfect entertaining drink as they can be made ahead and served in large pitchers full of ice—always welcome on a hot sunny afternoon.

Whichever recipe you make, start at the best source of ingredients, whether that's your local farmers' market or your very own plot. Either way, you are in the midst of the freshest seasonal fruits and vegetables in your area. Buying local sustainable produce is good for everyone in the community and tastes so much better than mass-market produce. Most of all you will enjoy the experience of canning, and especially the results to be enjoyed throughout the year.

PRESERVING *equipment*

Start with the right tools—you don't need a lot but there are few vital bits of equipment that make for successful canning.

Choose glass jars designed for canning in hot water or the oven. There are a few very good brands out there such as Ball, Kerr, and Mason, which come with lids that will seal easily. The size of fresh produce varies significantly from type and season so the size of jar you need may vary also.

Always ensure that the jars, bottles, and lids that you use are sterilized. To sterilize preserving jars, wash them in hot, soapy water and rinse in boiling water. Place in a large pot and cover with hot water. With the pot lid on, bring the water to a boil and continue boiling for 15 minutes. Turn off the heat and leave the jars in the hot water until just before they are to be filled. Invert the jars onto a clean dish towel to dry. Sterilize the lids for 5 minutes, by boiling or according to the manufacturer's instructions. If storing in a cupboard or pantry the jars must be sealed in airtight containers. Jars should be filled and sealed while they are still hot.

Invest in jar tongs—rubber tongs that are shaped to fit around the top of a glass canning jar. They will make it very easy for you to place the jars in boiling water and to remove them. A magnetic wand is a good thing to have on hand when sterilizing lids and bands in boiling water to make it easier to retrieve them without scalding yourself.

For preserving fruits and vegetables in jars it's best to use plastic or stainless steel wide-mouthed funnels, while narrow funnels are best for use when bottling.

A canning kettle is a good investment—large pots fitted with a metal rack in the bottom—but you can use any large pot with a metal rack placed in the bottom to ensure the jars sit away from direct heat. Have cooling racks laid out so you can remove and place the hot sealed jars onto them. This way they can cool completely without being disturbed.

Last, but not least, labels or pens that write on glass are invaluable. I know this seems a simple thing but once you start canning regularly and have a few different jars and bottles in your pantry, you might remember what is inside them but I promise, you will never remember the date that you made them.

SEALING *filled jars*

In order to store your preserves at room temperature you must first seal the jars to make them airtight. There are 2 ways to do this at home. They are both excellent and safe ways to seal your bounty but the key is to maintain a fixed temperature, which is easiest to control following the Water Bath Method. I tend to use the Oven Method when I am doing large amounts and the Water Bath Method for smaller batches. If the seal does not work following either method you can repeat the process, or simply store in the refrigerator.

NOTE: Preserving and canning at home carries some risks. For further information on food safety see page 4.

WATER BATH METHOD

Fill a canning kettle or large pot fitted with a metal rack on the bottom, with enough water to cover the height of the jars by 2 inches (5 cm) and bring to a boil.

Pack the fruit or vegetables into sterilized jars leaving space at the top according to the recipe. Screw the lids on, wipe the jars clean and, using jar tongs, place them in the water bath. Cover with a lid and once the water has come back to a boil seal for the specified time.

Remove the jars from the water bath using jar tongs and transfer to a cooling rack. Leave undisturbed until they have cooled completely—you will hear a pinging sound as each lids seals. Check to make sure that the center of the lid is concaved. Label and store.

OVEN METHOD

Heat the oven to 250°F (120°C) Gas ½.

Pack the fruit or vegetables into sterilized jars leaving space at the top according to the recipe. Screw the lids on, wipe the jars clean and, using jar tongs, place them in an ovenproof baking dish. Seal in the preheated oven for the specified time.

Remove the dish from the oven and, using jar tongs, transfer the jars to a cooling rack. Leave undisturbed until they have cooled completely—you will hear a pinging sound as each lids seals. Check to make sure that the center of the lid is concaved. Label and store.

PICKLING & VINEGARS

Pickling is like alchemy. It seems that you can pickle anything and use as many different sugars, sweeteners, spices, and vinegars as you wish and the outcome is always great: crunchy vegetables or fruit contained in wonderful flavorful brines. Once all the pickles are eaten, the brine can be used to flavor meat, fish, poultry, marinades, sauces, dressings, and cocktails, to name a few.

Pickles have been a part of household pantries for centuries. Historians believe the first pickling was done in the Tigris Valley with cucumbers that arrived from India. The Americas may not have been discovered if Columbus had not loaded up a precious cargo of pickles to prevent scurvy in the crew. The Roman army drank pickle juice to fortify their strength, and Cleopatra attributed her beauty to them.

Before refrigeration, pickling was a way to preserve the summer harvest produce for the winter months. Buying in bulk from farmers at the market does give you a great discount and helps build up a relationship with the growers. Of course, you can always grow and pick your own as well, which makes for a regular day in the garden or a nice day out in the countryside. Choose organic, sustainable produce and, most importantly, buy vegetables and fruits that are grown locally and are in season.

The yields in the recipes throughout the book are achievable, so if it's your first time canning you won't be overwhelmed with a kitchen full of market produce or get yourself in a pickle. A fun way to put your preserves to good use is to throw a canning party. Gather a few friends together and swap recipes.

It's a great way to lighten the load and everyone goes home happily with a jar of pickles under their arm.

Use tea, vinegars, agave, honey, flavored sugars, all kinds of spices, and herbs to flavor pickling brines—it's your chance to customize your jar and make it your own.

A good tip for deciding on the size of jar, and how many you are going to use, is to place the fruits or vegetables in the jars to measure them before you start pickling. This way you won't come up short or have too many jars. Use wide-mouthed jars so that you won't be squashing produce into the jar. For pickling, only use firm, fresh produce with no blemishes or bruises.

Most of the gourmet vinegars you see at your local market are expensive, but you can create a kaleidoscope of your own for very little money and with great ease. Use produce that's in season to get the maximum flavor. Spring and summer bring all the wonderful herbs, fruits, and summer vegetables. Fall/autumn reaps root vegetables, pears, and apples. In the depths of winter, citrus arrives like a sunburst and reminds us of the summer to come.

Store vinegars in sterilized bottles; these could be re-purposed wine bottles or condiment bottles. They can also be kept in glass jars with screw-top lids in a cool, dark place or in the refrigerator. Mix and match fruits, freshly picked herbs, and ground spices to flavor the vinegar.

Remember to label and date your jars and bottles, as you might forget what's in them, and then it becomes a lucky dip when you open them up.

Garden Patch PICKLES

a bunch of radishes, halved lengthwise

a bunch of baby carrots

½ cup/50 g pickled cornichons/mini gherkins

1 garlic clove, thinly sliced

3 celery stalks, cut in thirds

1 red onion, sliced

4 Persian cucumbers, quartered

a bunch of pencil-thin asparagus

4 cups/950 ml red wine vinegar

½ cup/110 g brown sugar

1 tablespoon mustard seeds

1 tablespoon fennel seeds

1 tablespoon cumin seeds

1 tablespoon dried rosemary

sterilized glass jars with airtight lids

MAKES 8 CUPS (64 OZ.)/1.8 L

I call this Garden Patch as these ingredients are very standard vegetables that work really well together when pickled. They stand up to strong spices and make nice, crunchy pickles to serve with Rillettes (see page 17), charcuterie, and cheese.

Pack all the vegetables into sterilized, size-appropriate glass jars leaving ½-inch (1-cm) space at the top.

Put the vinegar, sugar, mustard, fennel, cumin, and rosemary in a non-reactive pan and bring to a boil over medium heat. Turn down the heat and stir for 8–10 minutes until the sugar has dissolved.

Pour the hot vinegar mixture over the vegetables and carefully tap the jars on the counter to get rid of any air pockets. Wipe the jars clean and tightly screw on the lids. Turn the jars upside down and leave until completely cooled. Store in the refrigerator for at least 24 hours before serving. The pickles can be stored in the refrigerator for up to 2 months.

Springtime Pickled GREEN TOMATOES

In springtime when fresh garlic starts appearing at the farmers' market so, too, do the season's first green tomatoes. The two are a pickle dream.

Put the vinegar, sugar, mustard seeds, and green peppercorns in a non-reactive pan and bring to a boil over medium heat. Turn down the heat and stir for 8–10 minutes until the sugar has dissolved.

Pack the tomatoes and garlic into warm, sterilized, size-appropriate glass jars, leaving a ½-inch (1-cm) space at the top. Pour over the hot vinegar mixture and carefully tap the jars on the counter to get rid of any air pockets. Wipe the jars clean and screw on the lids. Seal the jars for 20 minutes following the Oven Method or 10 minutes following the Water Bath Method (see page 9). Once sealed, store unopened in a cool, dark place for up to 12 months.

COOKS' NOTE: To quick seal, screw on the lids and turn the jars upside down to cool completely, then store in the refrigerator for up to 2 months.

3 cups/700 ml apple cider vinegar

¾ cup/150 g turbinado/demerara sugar

1½ teaspoons mustard seeds

1½ teaspoons green peppercorns

4 large green tomatoes, quartered or sliced

2 garlic stalks, cut in half lengthwise

still-warm sterilized glass jars with airtight lids

MAKES 8 CUPS (64 OZ.)/1.8 L

Pickled CUCUMBERS

Pickled cucumbers go with absolutely everything, and yes, I have been known to dive into a jar armed only with a fork to scoop out those spicy, crunchy discs.

Rinse and slice the cucumbers into ½-inch (1-cm) rounds or cut into spears. Pack them into warm, sterilized, size-appropriate glass jars, leaving a ½-inch (1-cm) space at the top.

Place the salt, sugar, za'atar, peppercorns, vinegar, and 1 cup (235 ml) water in a non-reactive pan and bring to a boil. Reduce the heat and simmer for 6–8 minutes until the sugar has dissolved.

Pour the hot vinegar mixture over the cucumbers and carefully tap the jars on the counter to get rid of any air pockets. Wipe the jars clean and screw on the lids. Seal the jars for 20 minutes following the Oven Method, or 10 minutes following the Water Bath Method (see page 9). Once sealed, store unopened in a cool, dark place for up to 12 months.

10 Persian cucumbers

2 tablespoons salt

3 tablespoons sugar

2 teaspoons za'atar spice blend

2 teaspoons mixed whole peppercorns

3 cups/700 ml rice wine vinegar

still-warm sterilized glass jars with airtight lids

MAKES 4 CUPS (32 OZ.)/950 ML

Pickled GREEN TOMATO
PANZANELLA

¼ cup/60 ml Chive Blossom Vinegar (see page 34)

¼ cup/60 ml extra virgin olive oil, plus extra for the croutons and to serve

1 garlic clove, finely minced

sea salt and cracked black pepper, plus extra to serve

1½ cups/250 g heirloom/heritage cherry tomatoes, halved

1 cup/100 g Springtime Pickled Green Tomatoes (see page 13)

1 cup/15 g basil leaves, roughly torn

1 small red onion, thinly sliced

1 tablespoon capers

CROUTONS

6 thick slices ciabatta bread

2 garlic cloves, peeled

SERVES 4–6

Panzanella is the perfect answer for using up day-old bread. It just gets better as it sits and soaks up all the vinegars and pickled brine. Make it for supper or outdoor lunches—it is great as a picnic food as it transports so easily in containers.

Preheat a grill pan/griddle over medium–high heat.

Begin by preparing the croutons. Brush the sliced bread with olive oil and cook in the hot pan until golden and slightly charred on both sides. When toasted, set aside to cool, then rub all over with the garlic cloves. Roughly chop the toast into 1-inch (2.5-cm) croutons.

Put the Chive Blossom Vinegar and olive oil in a large bowl and whisk together. Add the minced garlic and season with salt and pepper. Add the croutons, heirloom/heritage cherry tomatoes, Pickled Green Tomatoes, basil, onion, and capers, and mix together. Cover and set aside for at least 1 hour before serving.

Spoon the Panzanella onto a serving dish. Drizzle with a little extra olive oil, sprinkle with salt and pepper, and serve immediately.

COOKS' NOTE: If desired, you can also add fresh mozzarella and a variety of soft green herbs, such as flat leaf parsley, to the Panzanella.

RILLETTES

with Garden Patch PICKLES

Rillettes are not just for the cold winter months or the holidays. A great year-round pantry staple for easy entertaining, just serve with pickles, crusty bread, and wine. I braise the meat in the oven to deepen the flavors.

Preheat the oven to 325°F (160°C) Gas 3.

Roughly cut the pork side/belly and shoulder into 2–2½-inch (5–7-cm) pieces and put in a 5-quart (5.5-litre) cast-iron pan with a tight-fitting lid.

Add the brandy, garlic, peppercorns, bay leaves, rosemary, thyme, allspice, orange peel, salt, and pepper. Pour over 4 cups (950 ml) cold water, making sure the meat is covered. Stir, cover, and cook in the pre-heated oven for 4 hours.

Remove the pork from the oven and drain into a colander set over a bowl to catch the cooking juices. Remove the herbs and peel and return the pork to the pan. Gently shred the pork using two forks. Add ⅔ cup (150 ml) of the reserved cooking juices and stir. Adjust the seasoning to taste and stir again to mix well.

Spoon the shredded pork into individual serving dishes or sterilized, size-appropriate glass jars and place a bay leaf on top. Let cool a little, then pour over enough melted butter to make a ½-inch (12-mm) seal in serving dishes or a 1-inch (2.5-cm) seal in jars. Screw the lids on tightly or cover with foil and refrigerate for 2 days before eating.

Serve with Garden Patch Pickles and sliced fresh bread.

COOKS' NOTE: You can also seal the rillettes with pork or duck fat in place of the melted butter. Jars can be stored in the refrigerator for 1 month.

2 lb./900 g pork side/belly

1 lb./450 g pork shoulder

¼ cup/60 ml brandy

4 garlic cloves, peeled and bashed

1 tablespoon green peppercorns

4 bay leaves, plus extra to garnish

1 sprig of fresh rosemary

6 sprigs of fresh thyme

1 tablespoon allspice

peel from 1 small orange

1 teaspoon sea salt, plus extra to taste

½ teaspoon ground black pepper

melted butter, to seal

TO SERVE

Garden Patch Pickles (see page 12)

sliced ciabatta bread

4 individual serving dishes or sterilized glass jars with airtight lids

SERVES 4

Pickled KAFFIR LIMES

24 small kaffir limes, quartered
12 kaffir lime leaves
2 cups/475 ml rice wine vinegar
2 tablespoons granulated/caster sugar
1 tablespoon kosher/rock salt
still-warm sterilized glass jars with airtight lids
MAKES 8 CUPS (64 OZ.)/1.8 L

Keep the pickling solution simple, as you want the wonderful floral aroma of the kaffir limes and leaves to sing. Add to crab cakes, pad thai, and anything you can think of—they are absolutely delicious!

Pack the limes into warm, sterilized, size-appropriate glass jars, leaving a ½-inch (1-cm) space at the top. Divide the kaffir leaves evenly between the jars.

Put the vinegar, sugar, and salt in a non-reactive pan and bring to a boil. Reduce the heat and simmer for 5 minutes until the sugar has dissolved.

Pour the hot vinegar mixture over the limes and carefully tap the jars on the counter to get rid of any air pockets. Wipe the jars clean and tightly screw on the lids. Turn the jars upside down to seal. Leave to cool completely, then store in the refrigerator for up to 12 months.

Indian PICKLED OKRA

1 lb./450 g okra, trimmed
6 garlic cloves, peeled and sliced
1 tablespoon curry powder
¼ teaspoon ground cinnamon
1 tablespoon green cardamom pods, bashed
2 tablespoons yellow mustard seeds
4 cups/950 ml apple cider vinegar
2 tablespoons dark brown sugar
still-warm sterilized glass jars with airtight lids
MAKES 6 CUPS (48 OZ.)/1.4 L

Love it or hate it, okra is definitely a great vegetable to pickle. These pretty, bright green spears are crunchy and bathed in wonderful Indian spices. Choose smaller okra, making sure it will fit in your glass jars.

Layer the okra with the garlic in warm, sterilized, size-appropriate glass jars leaving a ½-inch (1-cm) space at the top. Place the curry powder, cinnamon, cardamom pods, mustard seeds, vinegar, and sugar in a non-reactive pan and bring to a boil. Reduce the heat and simmer for 5 minutes until the sugar has dissolved.

Pour the hot vinegar mixture over the okra and carefully tap the jars on the counter to get rid of any air pockets. Wipe the jars clean and screw on the lids. Seal the jars for 30 minutes following the Oven Method or 15 minutes following the Water Bath Method (see page 9). Once sealed, store unopened in a cool, dark place for up to 12 months.

Pickled PEACHES with CHILE

Pickling peaches with these fiery chiles gives them a delightful punch. Chop the pickles up and turn them into a salsa, or blend into an ice-cold sorbet with a kick. The brine is also great to use in weekend party cocktails.

Put the vinegar, sugar, chiles, paprika, and raisins in a non-reactive pan and bring to a boil over a medium heat. Turn down the heat and stir the mixture for 5 minutes until the sugar has dissolved.

Pack the peach quarters into warm, sterilized, size-appropriate glass jars, leaving a ½-inch (1-cm) space at the top. Pour over the hot vinegar mixture and carefully tap the jars on the counter to get rid of any air pockets. Wipe the jars clean and screw on the lids. Seal the jars for 30 minutes following the Oven Method or 20 minutes following the Water Bath Method (see page 9). Once sealed, store unopened in a cool, dark place for up to 12 months.

COOKS' NOTE: To quick seal, screw on the lids, turn the jars upside down until completely cooled, then store in the refrigerator for up to 2 months.

8 firm, ripe peaches, peeled, stoned, and quartered

3 cups/700 ml apple cider vinegar

1½ cups/275 g granulated/caster sugar

1 habanero chile, finely sliced

3 small Serrano chiles, finely chopped

½ teaspoon smoked paprika

¼ cup/35 g (golden) raisins

sterilized glass jars with airtight lids

MAKES 6 CUPS (48 OZ.)/1.4 L

West Coast
CRAB CAKES

1 lb./450 g fresh crab meat

grated zest and freshly squeezed juice of 1 lemon

3/4 cup/180 g fresh corn kernels

2 scallions/spring onions, finely chopped

1 egg, lightly beaten

1 jalapeño chile, finely chopped

1 1/2 tablespoons Pickled Kaffir Limes
   (see page 18), finely chopped

sea salt and cracked black pepper, to taste

vegetable oil, for frying

COATING

1 egg, lightly beaten

2 cups fresh or Panko breadcrumbs

TO SERVE

fresh lime wedges

natural set yogurt

fresh green herbs, chopped

MAKES APPROXIMATELY 12

Crab cakes are best when using fresh crab meat. If it is not in season, buy good-quality canned crab meat. Pickled Kaffir Limes (see page 18) spice up the cakes and make them an enjoyable feast. Serve with herbed yogurt and citrus wedges for extra zing.

Mix together the crab meat, lemon zest and juice, corn, scallions/spring onions, egg, chile, and Pickled Kaffir Limes in a large mixing bowl. Season with salt and pepper.

For the coating, put the egg in a small, shallow bowl and the breadcrumbs on a plate. Shape a large tablespoon of the crab mixture into cakes with your hands. Dip each cake into the egg, then roll in the breadcrumbs.

Heat a skillet/frying pan over medium–high heat and drizzle with a little vegetable oil. Working in batches, sauté the crab cakes for 4 minutes on each side until golden brown, crispy, and cooked through. Transfer to a warm serving platter and serve with a squeeze of fresh lime and thick, creamy natural yogurt sprinkled with chopped green herbs.

Pickled ASPARAGUS

1 lb./450 g pencil-thin asparagus
1½ cups/350 ml red wine vinegar
1 teaspoon yellow mustard seeds
1 teaspoon mixed whole peppercorns
½ cup/100 g granulated/caster sugar
sterilized glass jars with airtight lids
MAKES 2 CUPS (16 OZ.)/475 ML

Choose a tall jar to pickle these asparagus spears—you want to keep them whole. Early, thin spring asparagus works well. They are great to eat as is, or mixed into salads and savory tarts.

Wash and trim the ends of the asparagus to fit in your glass jars, leaving a ½-inch (1-cm) space at the top and place inside with the tips facing up.

Place the vinegar, mustards seeds, peppercorns, and sugar in a non-reactive pan set over a medium–high heat and bring to a boil. Reduce the heat and simmer for 6–8 minutes or until the sugar has dissolved.

Pour the hot vinegar mixture over the asparagus and carefully tap the jars on the counter to get rid of any air pockets. Wipe the jars clean and screw the lids on. Seal the jars for 20 minutes following the Oven Method or 10 minutes following the Water Bath Method (see page 9). Once sealed, store unopened in a cool, dark place for up to 12 months.

Szechuan Pickled EGGS

12 eggs
2 teaspoons Szechuan seasoning
4–6 bay leaves
1 cup/235 ml apple cider vinegar
sterilized glass jar with airtight lid
MAKES 12

I love pickled eggs—they're such a great accompaniment to salads. Halve them, sprinkle with a dusting of black pepper and crunchy sea salt, and serve with chilled glasses of beer.

Bring a large pan of water to a boil, add the eggs, and boil for 10 minutes. Remove the eggs from the boiling water with a slotted spoon and put in a large bowl filled with ice cubes and water.

When the eggs are cold, peel and place in a large, sterilized glass jar. Add the Szechuan seasoning and bay leaves and pour over the vinegar. Screw the lid on tightly and store in the refrigerator for at least 1 month before eating. Once opened, keep refrigerated, and consume within 3 months.

COOKS' NOTE: To make saffron pickled eggs, omit Szechuan seasoning, add a pinch of saffron strands to the cider vinegar, and pour over the eggs. The saffron turns them a brilliant ochre colour and the flavor pairs well with Indian curries or Malaysian food.

Boozy BREAD & BUTTER PICKLES

I use smoked paprika with these pickles instead of the more classic turmeric. I like how it blends with the maple syrup and bourbon and gives a mellow flavor. Deck out a Bloody Mary (see page 26) with them.

Slice the cucumber into ¼-inch (5-mm) rounds. Layer the cucumber, shallots, garlic, chiles, and bay leaves into warm, sterilized, size-appropriate glass jars leaving a ½-inch (1-cm) space at the top. Place the paprika, allspice, mustard seeds, vinegar, bourbon, and maple sugar in a non-reactive pan set over a medium–high heat and bring to a boil. Reduce the heat and simmer for 8 minutes until the sugar has dissolved.

Pour the hot vinegar mixture over the vegetables and carefully tap the jars on the counter to get rid of any air pockets. Wipe the jars clean and screw the lids on. Seal the jars for 20 minutes following the Oven Method or 10 minutes following the Water Bath Method (see page 9). Once sealed, store unopened in a cool, dark place for up to 12 months.

6 medium-size cucumbers

2 shallots, thinly sliced

4 garlic cloves, peeled and quartered

4 red Serrano chiles, quartered

2 bay leaves

1 teaspoon smoked paprika

2 teaspoons allspice

2 tablespoons yellow mustard seeds

1½ cups/350 ml distilled white vinegar

½ cup/120 ml bourbon whiskey

½ cup/100 g maple sugar or granulated/caster sugar

still-warm sterilized glass jars with airtight lids

MAKES 8 CUPS (64 OZ.)/1.8 L

Spicy KIMCHI

You really can use any fruit or vegetable to make Kimchi. In Korean markets it is most often made with different kinds of cabbage. I sometimes make it with chard or kale and add Indian spices.

Cut the cabbages into 1-inch (2.5-cm) strips and put in a large ceramic bowl. Dissolve the salt in 6 cups (1.4 litres) water and pour over the cabbage. Cover with plastic wrap/clingfilm and let stand at room temperature for 8–24 hours.

Drain the cabbage and place back in the bowl with the carrots, scallions/spring onions, ginger, radishes, and cucumbers. Add the vinegar, fish sauce, Sambal Olek Chile Paste, and ½ cup (120 ml) water, and mix.

Spoon the cabbage mixture into sterilized, size-appropriate glass jars and pour over any remaining juice. Screw the lids on tightly and let the jars sit at room temperature for 24 hours. Refrigerate for at least 5 days before serving. The kimchi will keep in the refrigerator for up to 6 weeks.

1 small Napa cabbage, halved

1 small Savoy cabbage, halved and core removed

¾ cup/150 g sea salt

3 medium carrots, grated

4 scallions/spring onions, thinly sliced

a 2-inch/5-cm piece of ginger, peeled and grated

4 radishes, grated

2 Persian cucumbers, grated

½ cup/120 ml rice wine vinegar

2 tablespoons fish sauce

2 tablespoons Sambal Olek Chile Paste (see page 56)

sterilized glass jars with airtight lids

MAKES 4 CUPS (32 OZ.)/950 ML

Spicy KIMCHI
HASH BROWNS
with POACHED EGGS

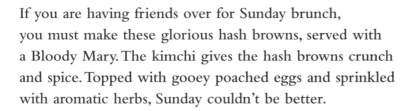

If you are having friends over for Sunday brunch, you must make these glorious hash browns, served with a Bloody Mary. The kimchi gives the hash browns crunch and spice. Topped with gooey poached eggs and sprinkled with aromatic herbs, Sunday couldn't be better.

Place the grated potato, garlic, and kimchi in a large bowl and mix together. Season with salt and pepper.

Heat a large cast-iron skillet/frying pan over medium–high heat and add the olive oil. When the oil starts to sizzle, add the potato-kimchi mix and brown for 2 minutes. Reduce the heat and continue to cook, stirring occasionally, for another 6–8 minutes. You want the hash browns to be crispy and browned.

Crack the eggs into separate small bowls. Fill a medium skillet/frying pan three-quarters of the way up with water. Add a tablespoon of vinegar and place over medium heat until bubbles start to form in the bottom. Carefully pour the eggs one at a time into the water, making sure they are spaced apart. Cook for 4 minutes, then remove with a slotted spoon, gently shaking off any excess water. Rest on a large plate.

Divide the hash browns between 4 plates or serving skillets (as shown) and top each with an egg. Sprinkle with torn Thai basil and parsley leaves. Drizzle with a little olive oil and finish with a sprinkle of salt and pepper. Serve with Texan Hot Sauce for a tangy kick.

1 large Russet potato, washed and grated, skin on

2 garlic cloves, finely minced

2 cups/160 g Spicy Kimchi (see page 23)

3 tablespoons olive oil, plus extra to serve

4 eggs

1 tablespoon vinegar

a bunch of Thai basil or regular basil, torn

a small bunch of flat leaf parsley, torn

TO SERVE

sea salt and cracked black pepper
Texan Hot Sauce (see page 44)

SERVES 4

The Ubiquitous
BLOODY MARY

4 cups/950 ml fresh tomato juice

1 cup/235 ml lemon vodka

1 teaspoon grated fresh horseradish

2 teaspoons Worcestershire sauce

grated zest and freshly squeezed
juice of 1 lemon

1 teaspoon celery salt

2 cups ice cubes

sea salt and cracked black pepper, to taste

Boozy Bread & Butter Pickles (see page 23),
to serve

a food processor

4–6 tall glasses, rim dipped in lemon juice then
celery salt

SERVES 4–6

It is hard to beat a wonderfully spicy, tomato Bloody
Mary. I have seen them served simply with a celery stalk
or extravagantly with slices of bacon and even shrimp/
prawns popping up over the edge of the glass. I serve
them with Boozy Bread & Butter Pickles (see page 23)
and dream of a lazy afternoon.

Place the tomato juice, vodka, horseradish, Worcestershire sauce, lemon
zest and juice, celery salt, and ice cubes in a food processor and blend
until smooth. Season with sea salt and pepper to taste.

Pour into tall glasses and serve with Boozy Bread & Butter Pickles.

COOKS' NOTE: To make 4½ cups/1 litre of homemade tomato juice, simply
blend 6 cups/900 g fresh tomatoes.

Pickled ROSE PETALS

What in life is better than champagne and roses? These pretty pickled petals make any dish or drink look glamorous and add a wonderfully heady floral flavor.

Place the rose petals in a ceramic bowl.

Put the champagne vinegar into a non-reactive pan over low heat and warm through. Take care not to boil the vinegar as it will damage the delicate petals. Remove from the heat and add the rose water. Cool for 5 minutes, then pour over the petals. Cover and leave to pickle overnight.

COOKS' NOTE: To make Rose Petal Vinegar, leave the rose petals in the vinegar in cool, dark place or a refrigerator for at least 5 days–1 month. Strain through cheesecloth/muslin and store in sterilized glass bottles.

petals of 8 small edible roses (about 3 cups/ 60 g petals), rinsed
2 cups/475 ml champagne vinegar or white wine vinegar
2 drops rose water (optional)

MAKES 4 CUPS (32 OZ.)/950 ML

Chilled PEAR YOGURT
with Pickled ROSE PETALS

This is a bright and lively soup, which I serve in small glasses as an appetizer. Adding the rose petals not only makes it look gorgeous, but also complements the gentle taste of the pears.

Place all the ingredients apart from the rose petals in a food processor and blend until smooth. Pour into glasses filled with ice and top with the pickled rose petals. Serve immediately.

COOKS' NOTE: Replace the pears with apples, nectarines, or peaches, depending on what is in season.

3 pears, cored, skin on
32 oz/950 ml plain full-fat yogurt
2 tablespoons clear honey
2 cups ice cubes
a pinch of salt
Pickled Rose Petals (see above), to garnish

a food processor

SERVES 6–8

Farmhouse GOAT YOGURT
with Pickled ROSE PETALS

Goat yogurt makes a refreshingly light dip and is perfect as a snack with flatbreads. It goes really well with Indian and Mediterranean foods too. The rose petals add a vibrancy to the dip and make it look almost too good to eat.

Line a strainer/sieve with cheesecloth/muslin or a coffee filter. Rest over a bowl deep enough to hold the drained whey. Pour the yogurt into the lined strainer/sieve, cover, and refrigerate overnight.

When ready to serve, remove the yogurt from the refrigerator and place in a bowl. Stir in the lemon zest and season with salt and pepper. Sprinkle with pickled rose petals and drizzle with olive oil. Serve with cheese straws, grilled pitas, or crudités.

COOKS' NOTE: Save the reserved whey for making protein-rich smoothies.

32 oz/950 ml full-fat goat yogurt
grated zest of 1 lemon
sea salt and cracked black pepper, to taste
Pickled Rose Petals (see page 29)
extra virgin olive oil, to drizzle

SERVES 4–6

Chive Blossom VINEGAR

a bunch of chive blossom, rinsed

4 cups/950 ml rice wine vinegar

a large sterilized glass jar and sterilized bottles with airtight lids

MAKES 4 CUPS (32 OZ.)/950 ML

Chives were among one of the first herbs that I grew as a child in my little patch of the family garden. The blossoms are so pretty, especially torn up and sprinkled over salads. Even better, they make a vibrant pink vinegar that adds gusto to any dish.

Place the rinsed chive blossom in a large sterilized glass jar.

Put the vinegar in a non-reactive pan and bring to a boil over medium heat. Pour over the blossoms, allow to cool, and cover.

Place in cool, dark place or a refrigerator for 5 days–1 month. Strain the vinegar through a cheesecloth/muslin or coffee filter and decant into sterilized bottles. Store in the refrigerator for up to 12 months.

Tarragon VINEGAR

Tarragon is one of my all-time favorite herbs and I feel it often gets forgotten. It has such a fantastic liquorish taste and its pretty, wavy leaves look great as a garnish or stirred into soups and stews.

Pull the leaves off the tarragon stems and rinse in a strainer/sieve under cold water. Roughly chop the leaves and place them a large sterilized glass jar. Add the fennel seeds.

Put the vinegar in a non-reactive pan and bring to a boil over medium heat. Pour over the tarragon, allow to cool, and cover.

Place in cool, dark place or a refrigerator for 5 days–1 month. Strain the vinegar through a cheesecloth/muslin or coffee filter and decant into sterilized bottles. Store in the refrigerator for up to 12 months.

a bunch of tarragon, roughly chopped
1 teaspoon fennel seeds
2 cups/475 ml white wine vinegar

a large sterilized glass jar and sterilized bottles with airtight lids

MAKES 2 CUPS (16 OZ.)/475 ML

Meyer Lemon & Rosemary VINEGAR

Meyer lemons have a wonderful citrus perfume which works so well with rosemary that they are widely used in Mediterranean cooking. This is a lovely vinegar to pour over sliced apples or pears, which makes a grand addition to a cheeseboard.

Cut the lemons into ½-inch (1-cm) slices. Place them along with the rosemary in a large sterilized glass jar.

Put the vinegar in a non-reactive pan and bring to a boil over medium heat. Pour over the lemons, allow to cool, and cover.

Place in cool, dark place or a refrigerator for 5 days–1 month. Strain the vinegar through a cheesecloth/muslin or coffee filter and decant into sterilized bottles. Store in the refrigerator for up to 12 months.

2 large Meyer lemons
a small sprig of rosemary
4 cups/950 ml apple cider vinegar

a large sterilized glass jar and sterilized bottles with airtight lids

MAKES 4 CUPS (32 OZ.)/950 ML

Raspberry VINEGAR

3–3 ¼ cups/450 g raspberries, rinsed

4 cups/950 ml red wine vinegar

a large sterilized glass jar and sterilized bottles with airtight lids

MAKES 4 CUPS (32 OZ.)/950 ML

You can buy fruit vinegars very easily, but they are often expensive. This only takes a moment to make and is a fabulous addition to your pantry. They also make great gifts for friends and family.

Place the rinsed raspberries in a large sterilized glass jar.

Put the vinegar in a non-reactive pan and bring to a boil over medium heat. Pour over the raspberries, allow to cool, and cover.

Place in cool, dark place or a refrigerator for 5 days–1 month. Strain the vinegar through a cheesecloth/muslin or coffee filter and decant into sterilized bottles. Store in the refrigerator for up to 12 months.

Blackberry VINEGAR

2 cups/260 g blackberries, rinsed

3 cups/700 ml white balsamic vinegar

a large sterilized glass jar and sterilized bottles with airtight lids

MAKES 4 CUPS (32 OZ.)/950 ML

You may be lucky and have blackberry bushes growing wild nearby, but if not, head to the farmers' market when they are in season. It makes the most gorgeous dark ruby-colored vinegar that is great for cocktails!

Place the rinsed blackberries in a large sterilized glass jar.

Put the vinegar in a non-reactive pan and bring to a boil over medium heat. Pour over the blackberries, allow to cool, and cover.

Place in cool, dark place or a refrigerator for 5 days–1 month. Strain the vinegar through a cheesecloth/muslin or coffee filter and decant into sterilized bottles. Store in the refrigerator for up to 12 months.

Lemon Verbena VINEGAR

I am really lucky to have a lovely neighbor who has the most wonderful garden full of vegetables and fruit trees. She gave me a huge armful of lemon verbena, which filled the kitchen with the most amazing lemon aroma. I made tea with it, baked with it and marinated chicken in it, as well as making a lovely batch of vinegar.

Place the rinsed lemon verbena leaves in a large sterilized glass jar.

Put the vinegar in a non-reactive pan and bring to a boil over medium heat. Pour over the lemon verbena, allow to cool, and cover.

Place in cool, dark place or a refrigerator for 5 days–1 month. Strain the vinegar through a cheesecloth/muslin or coffee filter and decant into sterilized bottles. Store in the refrigerator for up to 12 months.

2 cups/40 g lemon verbena leaves, rinsed
4 cups/950 ml champagne or white wine vinegar

a large sterilized glass jar and sterilized bottles with airtight lids

MAKES 4 CUPS (32 OZ.)/950 ML

Lobster & Tarragon
POTATO SALAD

2 lobsters (about 2 lbs./900 g each),
  freshly cooked
1½ lbs./680 g baby potatoes
1 head frisée or endive/chicory
1 cup/20 g fresh tarragon leaves
2 tablespoons tarragon vinegar
2 tablespoons mayonnaise
1 tablespoon Wholegrain Mustard (see page 65)
¼ cup/60 ml Extra Virgin olive oil
sea salt and cracked black pepper

SERVES 4

If I could eat lobster every day I would, in any shape
or form. For me there is nothing better in the world
than freshly cooked lobster and a glass of very cold
white wine. This is a delicate salad perfumed with
tarragon, perfectly matched for summer eating.

Crack the shell of the lobsters and pull out all the meat. Place in a large
bowl and break the meat in to large chunks.

Steam the potatoes over a large pot of boiling water for 10–15 minutes
or until a sharp knife easily pierces through them. Rinse the frisée or
endive/chicory in cold water and dry it. Tear the leaves and set aside.

In a large serving bowl whisk together the vinegar, mayonnaise, and
mustard. Pour in the olive oil and whisk to combine. Season with salt
and pepper.

Add the lobster, warm potatoes, frisée or endive/chicory, and tarragon
leaves. Toss together, sprinkle with cracked black pepper, and serve.

COOKS' NOTE: Reserve the lobster heads and shells to make fish stock.

Blackberry VINEGAR
STRAWBERRIES
with LAVENDER SHORTBREADS

I'm sure everyone has tossed unripe or not very sweet strawberries in balsamic vinegar with a little sugar to make them taste delicious. Try it with different flavored vinegars and use ripe, sun-kissed strawberries to make it taste even better.

Rinse the strawberries under cold water and cut them in half if they are very large. Place in a bowl and pour over the Blackberry Vinegar. Sprinkle with granulated/caster sugar, gently toss together, and set aside to marinate for 1–2 hours at room temperature.

To make the shortbread, preheat the oven to 375°F (190°C) Gas 5. In an electric stand mixer, cream the butter and superfine/caster sugar together until light and fluffy. Slowly add the all-purpose/plain flour until completely mixed. Turn the dough out onto a lightly floured surface and roll into a sausage shape. Wrap in plastic wrap/clingfilm and place in the freezer for 15 minutes.

To make the lavender sugar, mix the lavender flowers and superfine/caster sugar together in a small bowl.

Remove the dough from the freezer and cut into discs about ¼ inch (5 mm) thick. Place on the prepared baking sheet and sprinkle lightly with the lavender sugar. Bake for 6–8 minutes until golden.

Remove from the oven and sprinkle again with a little more lavender sugar. Serve the strawberries with crème fraîche in bowls and a stack of lavender shortbreads on the side.

4–4 ½ cups/450 g ripe strawberries, hulled
¼ cup/60 ml Blackberry Vinegar (see page 36)
1 tablespoon granulated/caster sugar
crème fraîche, to serve

SHORTBREAD PASTRY

2 sticks/225 g butter, room temperature
²/₃ cup/125 g superfine/caster sugar
1 cup/125 g all-purpose/plain flour

LAVENDER SUGAR

2 tablespoons edible lavender flowers
3 tablespoons superfine/caster sugar

an electric stand mixer
1 baking sheet lined with baking parchment
SERVES 4–6

RELISHES & MUSTARDS

I can't imagine eating a hot dog, burger, or gooey grilled cheese sandwich without lashings of spicy relishes and mustards. It's the best part.

Relishes, which fall somewhere between pickles and chutneys, are wonderful condiments that brighten up all kinds of foods. They can be simple or complicated, fresh or cooked, spiced or herbed, chunky or smooth, and each has its own unique taste. As with pickles, you really can mix and match ingredients for delicious results by using the freshest and ripest fruits and vegetables from a local source. They dress up leftover turkey sandwiches during the holiday season, are great slathered between thick, freshly sliced pieces of bread—their tart and zesty flavors brighten each mouthful, proudly sit alongside roasted and grilled meats, perk up pizzas, and top many a perfectly pan-roasted fish.

Each country and culture has its own mainstay relish used in its cooking, such as Sambal Oelek Chile Paste (page 56) from Malaysia, served as it comes and stirred it into soups or noodles to add a little heat. Tangy Nectarine Agrodolce (page 51) brings Italy to your kitchen. It is the Italian version of sweet and sour sauce, and can be served warm or cold with chicken or fish dishes. The Great British Piccalilli (page 50), served with ploughman's lunches and cold pork pies, is a staple of pub culture, and its wonderfully vivid and bright turmeric color adds a flavor of India.

I like to pack my relishes into small glass jars, as that way I can have several open at once—this works well for a casual get-together. Create a voluptuous cheeseboard and serve with an array of relishes.

Mustard is a very busy condiment in the kitchen —the little seeds have been popular for centuries. Punchy, robust, and flavorsome, we whisk it into vinaigrettes, marinades, rubs, sauces, and glazes, to name just a few. Known for its medicinal qualities, it can help cure a sore throat, take the pain out of an insect bite or sting, and even be used as a face mask.

Every possible flavor of mustard lines the shelves of grocery stores, and commands a high price tag. However, making your own is quick and simple. Soak yellow or brown mustard seeds in vinegar, pulse in a food processor, and as easy as that you'll have your very own homemade mustard. You can be a purist and keep them very simple or add spices, herbs and citrus to create your own gourmet mustard. Or you can even do as the Romans did, making mustard with wine.

Whether grainy or smooth, mustards take exceptionally well to alcoholic flavoring, adding bourbon, whiskies, ports, beers, and liqueurs. These bold flavors are especially tasty on grilled steak or pulled pork sandwiches. Or you can take a spoonful and stir it into creamy mayonnaise to instantly create a wonderfully delicious dip for crispy fried seafood or potato fries.

Mustards do not need to be sealed as pickles do, and they will keep refrigerated for up to 2 months. You can re-purpose jars but make sure they are sterilized and have tight-fitting lids. You will be as keen as mustard to make more!

Texan HOT SAUCE

16 fresh red jalapeño chiles, stems removed

14 garlic cloves, peeled and bashed

3 tablespoons vegetable oil

1 tablespoon smoked paprika

2 tablespoons ancho chiles in adobo sauce

¼ cup/85 g honey

¼ cup/60 ml rice wine vinegar

¼ cup/55 g dark brown sugar

sterilized glass jars or bottles with airtight lids

MAKES 2 CUPS (16 OZ.)/475 ML

Great food can be found in Texas, and they're not afraid of using fiery-hot chiles to flavor up hunks of meat. Roasting the chiles and garlic deepens the flavor and adds sweetness, and this sauce gets better as it ages.

Preheat the oven to 375°F (190°C) Gas 5.

Place the jalapeños and garlic in a baking dish, drizzle with the oil and toss. Roast for 25–30 minutes, stirring halfway through. Remove from the oven and leave to cool before putting in a food processor. Add the paprika, ancho chiles, honey, vinegar, sugar and a little water, then blend until smooth.

Pour the mixture into a non-reactive pan and bring to a boil. Reduce the heat and simmer for 15 minutes until the color deepens. Pour into sterilized glass jars or bottles and carefully tap the jars on the counter to get rid of any air pockets. Wipe the jars clean and screw on the lids. Seal the jars for 30 minutes following the Oven Method or for 15 minutes following the Water Bath Method (see page 9). Once sealed, store unopened in a cool, dark place for up to 12 months.

Corn & Poblano RELISH

This relish is sweet and tangy and has a lot of spice. Delicious spooned over tacos, burgers, hot dogs, and any kind of grilled foods.

Place a lightly-oiled large cast-iron pan over high heat until smoking. Add the poblano chiles, lower the heat slightly, and cook until the skins are charred and blistered. Remove from the pan and set aside to cool.

Once cool, roughly chop the Poblano chiles and set aside. Return the pan to a medium heat and add the olive oil, garlic, red onion, and bell pepper, and sauté for 5 minutes. Add the chopped poblanos, corn kernels, scallions/spring onions, lime zest and juice, and Aleppo pepper, and stir. Add the sugar, pour in the vinegar and season with salt and pepper. Stir and bring to a boil, then reduce the heat and simmer for 15–20 minutes.

Pack the relish into warm sterilized glass jars, leaving a ½-inch (5-mm) space at the top. Carefully tap the jars on the counter top to get rid of air pockets. Wipe the jars clean and screw on the lids. Seal the jars for 15 minutes following the Oven Method or 10 minutes following the Water Bath Method (see page 9). Once sealed, store unopened in a cool, dark place for up to 12 months.

3 Poblano chiles

2 tablespoons olive oil, plus extra for oiling

2 garlic cloves, finely chopped

1 red onion, finely diced

1 red bell pepper, finely diced

3 ears of corn, kernels removed (approximately 3 cups/420 g kernels)

6 scallions/spring onions, thinly sliced

grated zest and freshly squeezed juice of 1 lime

1 tablespoon Aleppo pepper/Turkish chili flakes

¾ cup/150 g light brown sugar

1 ¾ cups/425 ml apple cider vinegar

sea salt and cracked black pepper

still-warm sterilized glass jars with airtight lids

MAKES 4 CUPS (32 OZ.)/950 ML

Smoky Mountain KETCHUP

Save this recipe for the heart of summer, when tomatoes are at their peak. Be warned, this is a fiery sauce. Reduce the amount of chipotle chile for a milder taste.

Put the oil, garlic, and onion in a large cast-iron pan over medium–high heat and sauté for 3–5 minutes until tender, golden, and translucent. Season with salt and pepper. Add the tomatoes, chipotle chiles, honey, and wine, and bring to a boil. Reduce the heat, and simmer for 45 minutes, stirring occasionally. Cook until the sauce has thickened and deepened in color. Remove from the heat and set aside to cool slightly.

Pour the sauce into a food processor and blend until smooth. Check the seasoning and adjust if necessary. Pour the ketchup into sterilized glass jars or bottles and carefully tap the jars on the counter to get rid of any air pockets. Wipe the jars clean and screw on the lids. Seal the jars 30 minutes following the Oven Method or 15 minutes following the Water Bath Method (see page 9). Once sealed, store as above for up to 12 months.

3 tablespoons olive oil

4 garlic cloves, peeled and bashed

1 medium- large yellow onion, roughly chopped

2 lbs./900 g very ripe tomatoes, roughly chopped

3 tablespoons chipotle chiles in adobo sauce

2 tablespoon honey

1 cup/235 ml red wine

sea salt and cracked black pepper

sterilized jars or bottles fitted with airtight lids

MAKES 4 CUPS (32 OZ.)/950 ML

EMPANADAS
with Texan HOT SAUCE

2 tablespoons olive oil

½ medium white onion, finely diced

2 garlic cloves, finely chopped

1 jalapeño chile, finely diced

8 oz./225 g ground/minced beef

2 teaspoons dried marjoram

2 teaspoons dried oregano

¼ cup/60 ml Provençal Olive Relish (see page 50)

1 teaspoon sweet paprika

½ cup/125 ml red wine

1 quantity Pastry (see page 86)

1 egg, lightly beaten

sea salt and cracked black pepper

Texan Hot Sauce (see page 44)

a 3 ½-inch/9-cm cookie cutter

a baking sheet lined with baking parchment

MAKES 28

These delicious little Spanish pastry parcels filled with herbed meat are fantastic to hand around at parties or barbecues. Bite-size and dipped in hot sauce, they are hard to resist.

Preheat the oven to 425°F (210°C) Gas 7.

Heat the olive oil in a skillet/frying pan over medium–high heat, add the onion, garlic, and jalapeño, and cook for 5 minutes until golden brown. Add the beef, marjoram, oregano, Provençal Olive Relish, paprika, and stir. Pour in the wine and cook for 8 minutes, stirring occasionally. Season with salt and pepper, remove the pan from the heat, and cool.

Roll out the pastry as thinly as possible on a lightly floured surface, and cut rounds of pastry with the cookie cutter. Gather the leftover pastry and repeat until all the pastry is used up. Place a teaspoon of the filling in the middle of each round. Fold over and seal the edges with a fork. Place them on the prepared baking sheet and brush with the beaten egg.

Bake in the oven for 15 minutes until golden brown. Sprinkle with sea salt and serve with Texan Hot Sauce.

COOKS' NOTE: Any leftover filling can be eaten dolloped on crusty bread.

Southern SHRIMP
HUSHPUPPIES
with Corn & Poblano RELISH

These are named after the tidbits hunters carry to hush their dogs while hunting. This is a much more glamorous version—I'm sure hunters would not go to all the expense and trouble of putting corn or shrimp/prawns in theirs. You will, however, be speechless eating them.

Place the cornmeal, flour, baking soda/bicarbonate of soda, baking powder, salt and pepper in a large bowl and mix together. Pour in the buttermilk and egg and mix together. Add the shrimp/prawns, corn kernels, onions, and jalapeño and mix well to combine all the ingredients.

Place a deep skillet/frying pan over medium–high heat and add enough oil to come three-quarters of the way up the pan. Heat the oil to 365°F (185°C). Using a small ice cream scoop, and working in batches, drop the hushpuppies into the hot fat. Sauté for 5 minutes or until golden and cooked through. Transfer each batch to a warm serving plate.

Sprinkle with coarse sea salt and serve with Corn & Poblano Relish.

1 cup/150 g cornmeal

2 tablespoons all-purpose/plain flour

¼ teaspoon baking soda/bicarbonate of soda

3 teaspoons baking powder

½ teaspoon kosher/rock salt

½ teaspoon ground white pepper

¾ cup/180 ml buttermilk

1 egg, lightly beaten

8 oz./225 g shrimp/prawns, deveined

1 cup/140 g fresh corn kernels

2 scallions/spring onions, thinly sliced

1 jalapeño, finely chopped

vegetable oil, for deep frying

TO SERVE

sea salt

Corn & Poblano Relish (see page 45)

an oil resistant thermometer

MAKES APPROXIMATELY 20

Provençal OLIVE RELISH

2 cups/200 g pitted Kalamata olives, drained
12 anchovy fillets
¼ cup/40 g capers, drained
grated zest and juice of 1 lemon
¼ cup/60 ml extra virgin olive oil,
    plus extra to cover
cracked black pepper
sterilized glass jars with airtight lids

MAKES 3 CUPS (24 OZ.)/700 ML

This is Provence in a jar! The olives are drenched in oil and spiced with capers and salty anchovies. It works perfectly on bruschetta, pizzas, crudités, and pickled eggs, or lightly spread on chicken before roasting in the oven.

Place all the ingredients in a food processor and blend until the mixture is almost smooth but still has some texture. Season with pepper.

Pack the tapenade into a sterilized glass jar and drizzle with a little olive oil to cover the surface. Store in the refrigerator for up to 6 months.

PICCALILLI

1 large cauliflower, chopped into small florets
3 medium zucchini/courgettes, finely diced
2 shallots, thinly sliced
1 medium yellow onion, thinly sliced
3 garlic cloves, finely chopped
⅓ cup/65 g salt
1 tablespoon ground ginger
1 tablespoon ground cumin
1 tablespoon brown mustard seeds
2 tablespoons turmeric
2 tablespoons English mustard powder
1 tablespoon chili powder
1 tablespoon curry powder
3 tablespoons cornstarch/cornflour
½ cup/100 g sugar
2½ cups/600 ml apple cider vinegar
still-warm sterilized glass jars with airtight lids

MAKES 8 CUPS (64 OZ.)/1.8 L

Piccalilli is a classic British pickle. Served in pubs alongside a ploughman's lunch or a pork pie, it is a staple condiment that never seems to tire. This wonderful sunny yellow pickle has won a place in people's hearts.

Place the cauliflower, zucchini/courgettes, shallots, onion, and garlic in a large bowl. Sprinkle with the salt, cover and set aside 12–14 hours or overnight.

Rinse the vegetables under cold water and return to the bowl. Place the ginger, cumin, mustard seeds, turmeric, mustard powder, chili, curry, cornstarch/cornflour, sugar, and vinegar in a non-reactive pan and bring to a boil over medium heat. Turn down the heat and stir the mixture continuously for 3–4 minutes until it thickens. Pour over the vegetables and toss to mix thoroughly.

Pack the piccalilli into warm sterilized glass jars, leaving a ½-inch (5-mm) space at the top, and carefully tap the jars on the counter to get rid of any air pockets. Wipe the jars clean and screw on the lids. Seal the jars for 15 minutes following the Oven Method or 10 minutes following the Water Bath Method (see page 9). Once sealed, store unopened in a cool, dark place for up to 12 months.

COOKS' NOTE: Add raisins and grated apple to the mixture to give it a sweeter taste, and serve it with a spicy curry.

Nectarine AGRODOLCE

Agrodolce is an Italian sweet-and-sour sauce. The basic combination is made up of vinegar and sugar. This can be achieved in many ways with different vinegars, honey, syrups, fruit, and onions.

Preheat a cast-iron pan over medium heat and pour in the oil. Swirl the pan to coat. Add the onion and cook for 6–8 minutes, stirring occasionally, until golden and tender.

Add the vinegar, maple syrup, and raisins, and simmer for 10–12 minutes, until the mixture is syrupy. Add the nectarine and cook for another 5 minutes. Season with salt and pepper.

Remove from the heat and set aside to cool at room temperature. Serve or store in a sterilized glass jar in the refrigerator for up to 4 days.

3 tablespoons olive oil

1 white onion, finely diced

1 cup/235 ml white wine vinegar

1/4 cup/85 g maple syrup

1/4 cup/35 g (golden) raisins

1/2 lb./225 g (about 2) ripe nectarines, finely diced

sea salt and cracked black pepper

sterilized glass jars with airtight lids

MAKES 2 CUPS (16 OZ.)/475

South of the Border MUSTARD

Chipotle chiles in adobo sauce give this mustard a definite south-of-the-border feel. It is especially good used in marinades for fajitas and tacos.

Dry-roast the mustard seeds in a hot pan over a high heat for 2 minutes. Place the roasted seeds and vinegar in a ceramic bowl and set aside to soak for 12–14 hours or overnight.

Pour the soaked mustard seeds, honey, and chipotles in a food processor and blend until smooth. Add a little more vinegar if the mix is a little thick. Season with salt.

Pour the mixture into sterilized glass jars and screw the lids on tightly. Store in the refrigerator for up to 2 months.

1 cup/150 g yellow mustard seeds

1 cup/235 ml cider vinegar

1/4 cup/ 85 g honey

2 tablespoons chipotle chiles in adobo sauce

a pinch of sea salt

sterilized glass jars with airtight lids

MAKES 2 CUPS (16 OZ.)/475 ML

Summer CHICKEN
with Nectarine AGRODOLCE

1 whole chicken, cut into 10 pieces
2 tablespoons Wholegrain Mustard (see page 65)
2 tablespoons za'atar spice blend
2 tablespoons clear honey
¼ cup/60 ml olive oil
¼ cup/60 ml red wine vinegar
1 teaspoon sea salt
cracked black pepper, for sprinkling
sesame seeds, to serve (optional)
Nectarine Agrodolce (see page 51), to serve

SERVES 6

Grilled chicken, marinated in za'atar spices, then cooked over hot coals, is a great treat. The sweet-and-sour taste of the Nectarine Agrodolce adds a delicious tart and sweet flavor to this dish.

Place the chicken pieces in a ceramic dish. In a small bowl whisk together the Wholegrain Mustard, za'atar spice blend, honey, oil, vinegar, and salt. Pour over the chicken and toss to make sure all the pieces are coated. Sprinkle with pepper, cover, and refrigerate for 6–24 hours.

Once marinated, remove the chicken from the refrigerator and bring to room temperature.

Place a grill pan over medium–high heat. Add the chicken skin-side down (or skin-side up if using a broiler/grill) and cook for 8 minutes. Turn the chicken, reduce the heat, and cook for a further 8–10 minutes, turning occasionally. Remove the chicken from the heat, cover, and set aside to rest for 10 minutes.

Sprinkle the grilled chicken pieces with sesame seeds and serve with hot or cold Nectarine Agrodolce.

PISSALADIÈRE
with Provençal OLIVE RELISH

3 cups/375 g plain/all-purpose flour

¼ oz./7 g active dry/fast action yeast

2 tablespoons fresh thyme leaves

½ teaspoon salt

1¼ cups/300 ml warm water

½ cup/125 ml olive oil, plus extra to serve

8 red onions, peeled and thinly sliced

Provençal Olive Relish (see page 50)

12–14 anchovy fillets

15 pitted black olives

fresh thyme sprigs, to garnish

a baking sheet, oiled

SERVES 6

I fell in love with pissaladière the first time I bit into a slice in the south of France. The saltiness of the anchovies and sweetness of the caramelized onions with olive relish is sensational.

Begin by making the dough. Place the flour, yeast, thyme, and salt in a ceramic bowl, and mix together. Stir in the water and ¼ cup (60 ml) oil until combined. Cover with paper towel or plastic wrap/clingfilm and set aside to rise for 2½–3 hours until it doubles in size.

To caramelize the onions, place a large skillet/frying pan over medium–low heat and add the remaining olive oil and the onions. Cook for about 25 minutes, stirring occasionally, until the onions are golden brown and soft. Set aside.

Preheat the oven to 500°F (260°C) Gas 10 or as high as it will go.

Oil a baking sheet and turn the risen dough onto it. Gently press the dough with palms of your hands, stretching it to the edges of the pan. Spread the onions over the dough and randomly dollop the Provençal Olive Relish on top. Arrange the anchovies and olives on top.

Bake in the preheated oven for about 15–20 minutes, until the dough is golden and crispy. Remove from the oven and slice into portions.

Serve garnished with sprigs of thyme and a drizzle of olive oil.

COOKS' NOTE: You can also cook the pissaladière on a very hot barbecue with a lid.

Cucumber, Lemon, & Mint RELISH

2 Persian cucumbers, finely diced

1 garlic clove, finely chopped

grated zest and juice of 1 lemon

1 cup/25 g torn fresh mint leaves

1 cup/25 g roughly torn flat leaf parsley leaves

¼ cup/20 g fresh Greek oregano leaves

¼ cup/60 ml olive oil

sea salt and cracked black pepper

sterilized glass jars with airtight lids

MAKES 2 CUPS (16 OZ.)/475 ML

I have fresh mint growing everywhere I can in the garden, so I use it in anything and everything. It's another fantastically quick and easy addition to the dinner table and works well with all meats, fish, and poultry.

Mix all the ingredients together in a bowl. Season with salt and pepper and stir, making sure everything is well combined.

Chill before serving and store in sterilized glass jars in the refrigerator for up to 1 week.

Sambal Oelek CHILE PASTE

1 lb./450 g fresh red Serrano chiles

1 cup/200 g cane sugar

1 cup/235 ml rice wine vinegar

4 garlic cloves, bashed

still-warm sterilized glass jars with airtight lids

MAKES 2 CUPS (16 OZ.)/475 ML

This Malaysian condiment is surprisingly quick and easy to make. The Serrano chiles can be replaced by any other type of fresh chiles, such as habaneros or jalapeños. Spoon into Asian soups or noodles to give a little punch.

Add all the ingredients into a food processor and blend until smooth.

Pour the paste into a non-reactive pan and bring to a boil over medium heat. Reduce the temperature and simmer for 15–20 minutes until it thickens and has deepened in color.

Pour the Sambal into warm sterilized glass jars, leaving a ½-inch (5-mm) space at the top, and carefully tap the jars on the counter to get rid of any air pockets. Wipe the jars clean and screw on the lids. Seal the jars for 15 minutes following the Oven Method or 10 minutes following the Water Bath Method (see page 9). Once sealed, store unopened in a cool, dark place for up to 12 months.

Blistered Jalapeño, Lime, & Tequila RELISH

Once you taste this divine relish you will be dolloping it on everything you can think of. Roasting the jalapeños and blistering the skins sweetens them and picks out a smoky flavor.

Place a lightly-oiled large cast-iron pan over high heat until smoking. Add the jalapeños, lower the heat slightly, and cook until the skins are charred and blistered. Remove from the pan and set aside to cool.

Add the oil, sliced onions, and garlic to the pan and cook over medium heat for 5 minutes, stirring occasionally. Season with salt to taste. Add the diced lime skin with the onion.

Roughly chop the cooled jalapeños and add to the pan along with the tequila, honey, and vinegar. Cook for a further 10 minutes, until the onions are golden brown and soft.

Pack the relish into warm sterilized glass jars, leaving a ½-inch (5-mm) space at the top, and carefully tap the jars on the counter to get rid of any air pockets. Wipe the jars clean and screw on the lids. Seal the jars for 15 minutes following the Oven Method or 10 minutes following the Water Bath Method (see page 9). Once sealed, store unopened in a cool, dark place for up to 12 months.

COOKS' NOTE: You can substitute the jalapeños for any kind of fresh chile.

3 tablespoons olive oil, plus extra for oiling

4 jalapeño chiles

1 red and 1 white onion, thinly sliced

3 garlic cloves, finely chopped

skin of 1 Pickled Kaffir Lime (see page 18), finely diced

2 tablespoons tequila

3 tablespoons clear honey

¼ cup/60 ml white wine vinegar

sea salt

still-warm sterilized glass jars with airtight lids

MAKES 2 CUPS (16 OZ.)/475 ML

Ouzo
LAMB PITAS
with Cucumber, Lemon, & Mint RELISH

As well as roasting, you can also throw this deliciously marinated piece of lamb on the grill, which gives a great charred and smoky flavor. Ouzo adds a subtle liquorish flavor to the meat, which is enhanced by the fennel.

Preheat the oven to 400°F (200°C) Gas 6.

Place the lamb in a roasting pan and, using a sharp knife, carefully score the skin diagonally.

In a small bowl, whisk together the ouzo, oil, rosemary, garlic, and fennel pollen.

Pour the marinade over the lamb, rubbing it all over and into the scored skin. Season with salt and pepper. Roast in the preheated oven for 45 minutes. Remove the lamb from the oven, cover, and set aside to rest for 10 minutes.

To serve, slice the lamb into thick pieces. Arrange on a platter along with a bowl of Cucumber, Mint, & Lemon relish and toasted pita bread.

a 2-lb./900-g piece boneless lamb shoulder
½ cup/125 ml ouzo
¼ cup/60 ml olive oil
2 tablespoons fresh rosemary leaves
4 garlic cloves, roughly chopped
1 teaspoon fennel pollen
sea salt and cracked black pepper
Cucumber, Lemon, & Mint Relish (see page 56)
6 pita breads, lightly toasted

SERVES 6

Grilled
HALLOUMI
with Blistered
Jalapeño, Lime, & Tequila RELISH

1 lb./450 g halloumi cheese
3 tablespoons olive oil
grated zest and juice of 2 limes
Blistered Jalapeño, Lime, & Tequila Relish
  (see page 57)
cracked black pepper, for sprinkling
extra limes, for squeezing

SERVES 6

Halloumi is a Cypriot cheese with a rich, salty flavor, and is perfect for broiling/grilling and pan frying. It has a mild taste so it works very well alongside strong flavors or sweet fruits, such as watermelon and figs.

Begin by preparing the halloumi. Slice the cheese into ¼-inch (5-mm) pieces. Place a cast-iron pan over medium–high heat and pour in the olive oil. Swirl the pan to coat. Working in batches, add the halloumi and sauté on each side for 2 minutes. Add a little lime zest and juice to the pan per batch. The halloumi will cook quickly, so keep an eye on it.

Transfer the cheese to a warm serving platter.

Place a teaspoon of relish on top of each piece of cheese. Sprinkle with cracked black pepper and finish with an extra squeeze of lime.

Serve immediately.

Garlic & Mango MADRAS RELISH

flesh of 1 ripe mango, skin and stone removed

1 red chile, finely diced

grated zest and juice of 1 lime

1 tablespoon grated fresh ginger

2 scallions/spring onions, thinly sliced

1 garlic clove, finely chopped

½ teaspoon Madras curry powder

¼ teaspoon smoked paprika

¼ cup/60 ml rice wine vinegar

1 tablespoon sesame oil

2 tablespoons peanut/groundnut oil

1 tablespoon fish sauce

sea salt, to season

sterilized glass jars with airtight lids

MAKES 1½ CUPS (12 OZ.)/350 ML

Vibrant and gutsy Madras curry powder livens up the mango medley in this quick and versatile relish. Serve with absolutely anything—it's especially good piled on top of fish tacos.

Begin by preparing the mango. Cut the flesh into ½-inch (5-mm) cubes and place in a bowl. Add the chile, lime zest and lemon juice, ginger, onions, garlic, curry powder, and paprika. Toss to combine.

In a separate bowl, whisk together the vinegar, sesame and groundnut oils, and fish sauce. Pour over the mango mix and stir well to coat. Season with salt and chill in the refrigerator before serving.

COOKS' NOTE: Store in sterilized glass jars in the refrigerator for up to 1 week.

Roasted SPICED PLUMS

12 green plums or pluots, stones removed and quartered

2 white onions, thinly sliced

4 garlic cloves, roughly chopped

2½ cups/500 g turbinado/demerara sugar

2 cinnamon sticks

4 small dried chiles

1 teaspoon chili powder

2 teaspoons curry powder

½ cup/70 g (golden) raisins

4 bay leaves

1 cup/235 ml apple cider vinegar

sterilized glass jars with airtight lids

MAKES 2 CUPS (16 OZ.)/475 ML

This is a fantastic recipe in which everything magically happens in the oven at once. It came about following an over-zealous visit to the market. I was overwhelmed with my bounty, so I decided it should all just go in a roasting pan in the oven to cook.

Preheat the oven to 400°F (200°C) Gas 6.

Place all the ingredients in a ceramic baking dish and stir well.

Roast the plum mixture in the oven for 45 minutes, stirring every 10 minutes. Remove from the oven and set aside to cool slightly.

Turn the oven down to 250°F (120°C) Gas ½.

Spoon the relish into sterilized glass jars and carefully tap the jars on the counter to get rid of any air pockets. Wipe the jars clean and screw on the lids. Seal the jars following the Oven Method for 15 minutes or the Water Bath Method for 10 minutes (see page 9). Once sealed, store unopened in a cool, dark place for up to 12 months.

Southern MUSTARD

1 cup/150 g yellow mustard seeds

1 cup/235 ml cider vinegar

¼ cup/85 g honey

½ cup/100 g roughly chopped Boozy Bread & Butter Pickles with juices (see page 23)

½ teaspoon turmeric

pinch of sea salt

sterilized glass jars with airtight lids

MAKES 2 CUPS (16 OZ.)/475 ML

Homemade mustard is a breeze. Enjoy mixing and matching different mustard seeds with spices and herbs to make your own unique mustard. I always dry-roast the mustard seeds before making mustard as it gives a nuttier flavor.

Dry-roast the mustard seeds in a hot pan over a high heat for 2 minutes. Place the roasted seeds and vinegar in a ceramic bowl and set aside to soak for 12–14 hours or overnight.

Pour the soaked mustard seeds, honey, pickles, and turmeric in a food processor and blend until just a little chunky. Add a little more vinegar if the mix is a little thick. Season with salt.

Pour the mixture into sterilized glass jars and screw the lids on tightly. Store in the refrigerator for up to 2 months.

Lemon & Dill MUSTARD

1 cup/150 g yellow mustard seeds
1 cup/235 ml lemon verbena vinegar
¼ cup/85 g clear honey
grated zest and juice of 1 lemon
¼ cup/10 g fresh dill, roughly chopped
a pinch of sea salt

sterilized glass jars with airtight lids
MAKES 2 CUPS (16 OZ.)/475 ML

Lemon and dill lend a delicate flavor to all things, especially mustard. Add a spoonful to pan-fried salmon to make a zingy accompanying sauce, or stir a spoonful into mayonnaise or crème fraîche to serve with burgers.

Dry-roast the mustard seeds in a hot pan over a high heat for 2 minutes. Place the roasted seeds and vinegar in a ceramic bowl and set aside to soak for 12–14 hours or overnight.

Put the soaked mustard seeds, honey, zest, lemon juice, and dill in a food processor and blend until smooth. Add a little more vinegar if the mix is a little thick. Season with salt.

Pour the mixture into sterilized glass jars and screw the lids on tightly. Store in the refrigerator for up to 2 months.

Rosemary & Thyme MUSTARD

1 cup/150 g yellow mustard seeds
1 cup/235 ml apple cider vinegar
¼ cup/85 g clear honey
1 tablespoon fresh rosemary leaves, chopped
2 tablespoons fresh thyme leaves
a pinch of sea salt

sterilized glass jars with airtight lids
MAKES 2 CUPS (16 OZ.)/475 ML

Rosemary and thyme bring a wonderful Mediterranean herbal flavor to mustard. This is perfect for spreading on Breakfast Country Biscuits (see page 68). I also spread this mustard over a whole chicken before roasting to add flavor to the skin.

Dry-roast the mustard seeds in a hot pan for 2 minutes. Place the roasted seeds and vinegar in a ceramic bowl and soak overnight.

Put the soaked mustard seeds, honey, and rosemary and thyme leaves in a food processor and blend until smooth. Add a little more vinegar if the mix is a little thick. Season with salt.

Pour the mixture into sterilized glass jars and screw the lids on tightly. Store in the refrigerator for up to 2 months.

Wholegrain MUSTARD

Good whole grain mustards can be hard to find and also a little expensive. This is really good basic recipe that you can add wines, spices and herbs too. Particularly good on a steak sandwich.

Dry-roast the mustard seeds in a hot pan for 2 minutes. Place the roasted seeds and vinegar in a ceramic bowl and soak overnight.

Put the soaked mustard seeds, honey, and garlic in a food processor and pulse until you have a grainy mustard. Add a little more vinegar if the mix is a little thick. Season with salt.

Pour the mixture into sterilized glass jars and screw the lids on tightly. Store in the refrigerator for up to 2 months.

½ cup/75 g yellow mustard seeds
½ cup/75 g brown mustard seeds
1 cup/235 ml red wine vinegar
¼ cup/85 g clear honey
1 garlic clove, finely chopped
a pinch of sea salt

sterilized glass jars with airtight lids
MAKES 2 CUPS (16 OZ.)/475 ML

Médoc MUSTARD

Médoc is a red wine from the Bordeaux region of France, and is a good, robust wine to use in mustards. You can really use any good red wine. Don't be tempted to use a cheap one—it won't work.

Dry-roast the mustard seeds in a hot pan for 2 minutes. Place the roasted seeds and vinegar in a ceramic bowl and soak overnight.

Put the soaked mustard seeds, wine, vinegar, honey, and garlic in a food processor and blend until smooth. Add a little more vinegar if the mix is a little thick. Season with salt.

Pour the mixture into sterilized glass jars and screw the lids on tightly. Store in the refrigerator for up to 2 months.

½ cup/75 g yellow mustard seeds
½ cup/75 g brown mustard seeds
¾ cup/180 ml Médoc or other red wine
¼ cup/60 ml red wine vinegar
¼ cup/85 g clear honey
2 garlic cloves, roughly chopped
a pinch of sea salt

sterilized glass jars with airtight lids
MAKES 2 CUPS (16 OZ.)/475 ML

CHICKEN TIKKA

BITES *with Garlic & Mango* MADRAS RELISH

These tikka bites are especially welcome in the summer. Thrown straight onto the grill or barbecue, they are ready in minutes. The lime leaves give a delightful floral fragrance to the dish.

Begin by preparing the chicken. Cut the chicken fillets into 1½-inch (3.5-cm) chunks. Thread a piece of chicken onto a soaked wooden skewer, then a lime leaf, and another piece of chicken. Take another wooden skewer and repeat until you have used up all of the chicken. Place the skewers in a large shallow bowl and set aside.

Put the chopped ginger and garlic, coconut oil, lime zest and juice, curry powder, chili, paprika, and cilantro/coriander leaves in a food processor. Blend until smooth.

Pour the curry sauce over the prepared chicken skewers, coating the meat. Cover and set in the refrigerator to marinate for 2–4 hours.

Light the grill or barbecue, or place a grill pan over medium–high heat. Place the skewers directly on the heat or in the grill pan and cook for 4 minutes on each side, until the chicken is cooked through.

Serve with lime wedges and Garlic & Mango Madras Relish.

1 lb./450 g chicken fillets

12 lime leaves

a 2-inch/5-cm piece of fresh ginger, peeled and roughly chopped

3 garlic cloves, peeled and roughly chopped

¼ cup/60 ml coconut oil or vegetable oil

grated zest and juice of 2 limes

1 tablespoon curry powder

1 teaspoon chili powder

½ teaspoon smoked paprika

½ cup/10 g cilantro/coriander leaves

TO SERVE

lime wedges

Garlic & Mango Madras Relish (see page 62)

12 wooden skewers, pre-soaked

MAKES 12 SKEWERS

Breakfast
COUNTRY
BISCUITS with HAM

2½ cups/190 g all-purpose/plain flour

1 tablespoon baking powder

1 teaspoon baking soda/bicarbonate of soda

1 teaspoon *herbes de provence*

1 stick/115 g cold unsalted butter, cubed

½ cup/45 g grated strong cheddar cheese

1 cup/235 ml cold buttermilk, plus extra for brushing

sea salt

a few sprigs of thyme, to garnish

FILLING

½ lb./225 g good-quality sliced ham

Rosemary & Thyme Mustard (see page 64)

a 3½-inch/9-cm cookie cutter

a baking sheet lined with baking parchment

MAKES 9

These fluffy biscuits are similar to scones and excellent at any time of the day. They also make a great picnic food for taking on camping trips. I like to fill them with a fried egg and bacon for a hearty winter brunch.

Preheat the oven to 425°F (210°C) Gas 7.

Put the flour, salt, baking powder, baking soda/bicarbonate of soda, and herbs in a food processor. Pulse a few times to combine. Add the cubed butter and blend until the mix resembles fine breadcrumbs. Add the cheese. Then, with the motor running, pour in the buttermilk and blend until the dough comes together. Add a little more milk if required.

Turn the dough out onto a lightly floured surface and knead into a ball. Roll out the dough to a thickness of ¾ inch (2 cm) and cut out biscuits using the cookie cutter. Bring any leftover dough back together, roll out, and repeat.

Place the biscuits on the prepared baking sheet, brush the tops with buttermilk, and sprinkle with salt and thyme. Bake in the oven for 12–15 minutes, until golden brown. Remove from the oven and set aside to cool slightly.

While still warm, cut the biscuits in half, and fill with the ham and a dollop of Rosemary & Thyme Mustard. Serve immediately.

BOTTLING FRUIT & VEGETABLES

Bottling is a really good excuse for me to catch up with friends. I end up buying crates of fruit and vegetables at my local farmers' market in the height of their season. Apart from the fantastic flavors, it's also the most economical time to buy, as the market stalls are groaning from the weight of the harvest. So I always need extra hands to help chop and bottle.

The one thing I really like about bottling is that you can keep it simple by just using a few ingredients, which allows you to adapt the fare to any recipe. Or you can bathe the fruits and vegetables in flavors that will just keep getting better as they sit. Use this chance to add whole sprigs of herbs to the jars, but not just the usual suspects like rosemary, and thyme—try some Asian favorites such as curry leaves, kaffir lime leaves, and lemongrass. They look great and taste even better.

My favorite part of it all is when everything is canned. The labels are on, and the glass jars are sitting in perfect rows on the kitchen shelf in all their splendor, just waiting to be opened to become part of something grander or eaten as they come. However you choose to enjoy them you will be very happy you did it.

I try to keep stone fruits and citrus whole, but the amount of space in the jars often dictates how the fruits are cut up. I use larger glass jars for these recipes. Fruits vary in size throughout their season so I tend to pick the smaller ones to bottle. Feel free to change up the recipes and chop the fruit and vegetables into wedges or chunks to fit more easily in the jars.

A very good tip is to cut out circles of waxed paper or baking parchment to place on top of the fruit inside the jar. The paper keeps the fruit and vegetables submerged in the bottling liquid, as whole fruits tend to bob up above the surface.

I like to label simply, and sometimes I use a pen that writes on glass to name and date the contents. If you are gifting jars, it's nice to get a little artistic with the labels. Dress the jars up by covering the lids with a little piece of cloth or paper tied with twine.

Jam Jar Crumbles (page 95) are a genius way to cook individual crumbles, the perfect way to transport them to the beach or country for picnics—just screw the lids and pack. Swap the cherries for any of the bottled fruit recipes; they all work really well with the crumble topping.

Dried fruits bottle very well, especially using liqueurs, brandy, bourbon whiskies, and robust wines. They can be quickly turned into a gorgeous, boozy Weekend Chocolate Cake (page 78) for the grown-ups, to be savored on a lazy, winter Sunday afternoon reading the newspapers.

When I have friends staying I like to make a big stack of buckwheat pancakes on Sunday morning and top them with Chai-Infused Pears (page 85). I pile the pancakes on a large serving platter and spoon over the warmed pears and syrup. Served with a big pot of coffee, I just let everyone dig in and serve themselves. Not a sound can be heard.

Roasted BELL PEPPERS

4 red and 4 yellow bell peppers, seeds removed and cut into strips

6 garlic cloves, thinly sliced

1 teaspoon peppercorns

2 tablespoons fresh rosemary

1 teaspoon dark brown sugar

½ cup/125 ml olive oil

¼ cup/60 ml balsamic vinegar

sea salt

still-warm sterilized glass jars with airtight lids

MAKES 4 CUPS (32 OZ.)/950 ML

Enjoy these peppers as part of an antipasto plate or mixed into salads. I like to top burgers and grilled cheese sandwiches with them—they add a delightful sweetness.

Preheat the oven to 375°F (190°C) Gas 5.

Place the strips of red and yellow bell peppers in a roasting pan. Add the garlic, peppercorns, rosemary, sugar, oil, and vinegar. Mix thoroughly and roast in the oven for 30–35 minutes, until the edges of the peppers have started to brown. Remove from the oven and turn the temperature down to 250°F (120°C) Gas ½.

Pack the peppers into warm, sterilized glass jars, leaving a ¼-inch (5-mm) space at the top. Carefully tap the jars on the counter top to get rid of air pockets. Wipe the jars clean and screw on the lids. Seal the jars for 20 minutes following the Oven Method or 10 minutes following the Water Bath Method (see page 9). Once sealed, store unopened in a cool, dark place for up to 12 months.

Yellow & Green ZUCCHINI

4 yellow and 4 green zucchini/courgettes

1 cup/235 ml apple cider vinegar

still-warm sterilized glass jars with airtight lids

MAKES 12 CUPS (96 OZ.)/2.8 L

Bottling the zucchini/courgettes simply and not using any herbs lets you cook with them in many different ways, allowing you to add spices or herbs later.

Slice the zucchini/courgettes into ¼-inch (5-mm) circles and pack into warm, sterilized glass jars, leaving a ½-inch (1-cm) space at the top.

In a non-reactive pan, bring the vinegar and 3 cups (700 ml) water to a boil over medium–high heat.

Pour the hot brine over the zucchini/courgettes and carefully tap the jars on the counter top to get rid of air pockets. Wipe the jars clean and screw on the lids. Seal the jars for 20 minutes following the Oven Method or for 10 minutes following the Water Bath Method (see page 9). Once sealed, store unopened in a cool, dark place for up to 12 months.

Haricots Verts with PICKLED ONIONS

This is one of my pickling cheats. I love pickled cocktail onions and eat them straight from the jar. But I find peeling pounds of tiny onions for bottling boring and fussy, so I use pre-pickled onions as a shortcut here.

Pack the haricots verts, cocktail onions, and bay leaves into sterilized glass jars, leaving a ½-inch (1-cm) space at the top.

In a non-reactive pan, bring the brine from the onions, vinegar, 3 cups (700 ml) cold water, peppercorns, Piri Piri rub, sugar, and mustard seeds to a boil over medium–high heat. Reduce the heat and simmer for about 8 minutes, until the sugar has dissolved.

Pour the hot brine over the packed vegetables and carefully tap the jars on the counter top to get rid of air pockets. Wipe the jars clean and screw on the lids. Seal the jars using for 20 minutes following the Oven Method or 10 minutes following the Water Bath Method (see page 9). Once sealed, store unopened in a cool, dark place for up to 12 months.

COOKS' NOTE: To make the Piri Piri rub, mix together 1 tablespoon of red pepper flakes, 1 tablespoon smoked paprika and 1 tablespoon tomato powder.

1 lb./450 g haricots verts (green beans), trimmed

1 lb./450 g pickled cocktail onions, drained and brine reserved

6 bay leaves

½ cup/125 ml red wine vinegar

1 tablespoon peppercorns

2 tablespoons Piri Piri rub (see Cooks' Note)

2 tablespoons brown sugar

2 tablespoons brown mustard seeds

sterilized glass jars with airtight lids

MAKES 4 CUPS (32 OZ.)/950 ML

SALAD NIÇOISE
with PICKLED EGGS

leaves of 1 head butter/round lettuce, rinsed

8 oz./225 g best-quality preserved tuna in oil

1 red onion, thinly sliced

1 cup/150 g Haricots Verts with Pickled Onions
(see page 73)

18 anchovy fillets

½ cup/65 g Niçoise olives

2 cups/340 g cherry tomatoes, halved

6 Szechuan Pickled Eggs (see page 22),
quartered

¼ cup/60 ml Tarragon Vinegar (see page 35)

½ cup/125 ml extra virgin olive oil

sea salt and cracked black pepper

SERVES 4

This is by no means a traditional Niçoise. Enjoy the pickle flavors alongside the tuna and crispy lettuce, grill up some thick crusty bread and dig in. Use the best tuna you can find.

To prepare the salad, tear the lettuce leaves and arrange them in a large shallow bowl. Add the tuna, onion, Haricots Verts with Pickled Onions, anchovies, olives, and tomatoes. Place the Szechuan Pickled Eggs on top.

Whisk together the vinegar and oil and season with salt and pepper.

Drizzle a little vinaigrette over the salad, gently toss, and serve immediately.

COOKS' NOTE: Reserve any extra vinaigrette for another use.

Market CORN & CHILES

12 ears of corn
  (approximately 2 cups/280 g kernels)
8 red jalapeño chiles
4 teaspoons white sugar
1 cup/235 ml red wine vinegar

sterilized glass jars with airtight lids

MAKES 8 CUPS (64 OZ.)/1.8 L

This is gold in a jar during the winter months: wonderful market corn and chiles for making crab cakes, corn fritters and spicy cornbread, perfect for brightening up any dark winter night.

Shuck the corn and run the blade of a sharp knife down the cobs to remove the kernels. Cut the jalapeños into quarters. Layer the corn and chiles in warm sterilized jars leaving a ½-inch (1-cm) space at the top.

In a non-reactive pan, bring the vinegar, 2 cups (475 ml) water, and sugar to a boil over medium-high heat. Reduce the heat and simmer for 5 minutes, until the sugar has dissolved.

Pour the hot brine over the corn and carefully tap the jars on the counter top to get rid of air pockets. Wipe the jars clean and screw on the lids. Seal the jars for 20 minutes following the Oven Method or for 10 minutes following the Water Bath Method (see page 9). Once sealed, store unopened in a cool, dark place for up to 12 months.

Provençal PEACHES with LAVENDER

In this dish, all the flavors of the south of France come together to brighten up a winter day when the thought of summer and the peach season is a distant memory. Eat the peaches just as they are or use them as fillings for cakes and tarts—either way, you won't be disappointed.

1½ cups/300 g superfine/caster sugar
25 oz./750 ml rosé wine
2 teaspoons edible lavender flowers
12 small firm white peaches, peeled

sterilized glass jars with airtight lids
MAKES 8 CUPS (64 OZ.)/1.8 L

Place the peeled peaches whole in warm, sterilized glass jars, leaving a ½-inch (1-cm) space at the top.

In a non-reactive pan, bring the sugar and wine to a boil over medium–high heat. Reduce the heat and simmer for 5 minutes, until the sugar has dissolved. Remove from the heat and stir in the lavender flowers. Set aside to cool for 5 minutes. Strain the syrup through a fine-mesh strainer/sieve.

Pour the syrup over the peaches and carefully tap the jars on the counter top to get rid of air pockets. Place a circle of parchment paper on top of the peaches to keep them submerged. Wipe the jars clean and screw on the lids. Seal the jars for 20 minutes following the Oven Method or for 10 minutes following the Water Bath Method (see page 9). Once sealed, store unopened in a cool, dark place for up to 12 months.

Armagnac PRUNES

This is a wonderful way of cooking with prunes, and is a classic dish from Southwest France. Armagnac is a sensational brandy from that region. They make fantastic pantry staples for rustling up a quick dessert.

3½ cups/450 g dried prunes
2 tablespoons brown sugar
1 cup/235 ml Armagnac or other brandy

sterilized glass jars with airtight lids
MAKES 2½ CUPS (18 OZ.)/500 G

Begin by preparing the prunes. In a non-reactive pan, bring the sugar and 2 cups (475 ml) of water to a boil over medium–high heat. Reduce the heat and simmer for 5 minutes, until the sugar has dissolved. Pour the syrup over the prunes in a large bowl, cover, and soak for 12–14 hours, or overnight.

Once soaked, remove the cover, and stir the Armagnac into the prunes in syrup. Pack the prunes into sterilized glass jars, leaving a ¼-inch (5-mm) space at the top. Carefully tap the jars on the counter top to get rid of air pockets. Wipe the jars clean and tightly screw on the lids. Store in the refrigerator for up to 12 months.

Weekend CHOCOLATE CAKE
with Armagnac PRUNES

8 eggs

1¼ cups/250 g light brown sugar

⅔ cup/85 g good-quality cocoa powder

1 cup/125 g all-purpose/plain flour

1 teaspoon pure vanilla extract

1 stick/115 g unsalted butter, melted

½ cup/120 g Armagnac Prunes (see page 77), finely chopped

mascarpone, to serve

SYRUP

¼ cup/55 g brown sugar

¼ cup/60 ml water

¼ cup/60 ml Armagnac

¼ cup/85 g honey

1 cup/225 g Armagnac Prunes (see page 77)

a 10-inch/25-cm springform cake pan, buttered and floured

an electric stand mixer fitted with a paddle attachment

a wooden skewer or toothpick/ cocktail stick

SERVES 6–8

This is a fun cake to make. Rich and decadent, and steeped in heavenly Armagnac syrup and prunes, it takes time to eat and savor—perfect for those long, lazy lunches.

Preheat the oven to 350°F (180°C) Gas 4.

Sift the cocoa and flour together into a large bowl, and set aside.

Place the eggs and sugar in a electric stand mixer and beat on high for 5–6 minutes until light and fluffy. Reduce the speed of the mixer to slow, and add the cocoa and flour a little at a time. Add the pure vanilla extract, butter, and chopped prunes, and mix until combined.

Pour the cake batter into the prepared cake pan and bake in the preheated oven for 35 minutes.

Check it is cooked through by inserting a wooden to skewer into the middle of the cake: if it comes out clean, it's ready. Remove the cake from the oven and let cool in the pan on a wire rack. Prick the top of the cake all over with a wooden skewer.

To make the syrup, bring the sugar, water, Armagnac and honey to a boil in a small saucepan over medium–high heat. Cook for 4–5 minutes, stirring occasionally, until it thickens. Pour the hot syrup over the cake, cover, and set aside at room temperature for 12–14 hours or overnight.

The next day, remove the cake from the pan and place on a serving plate. Top with the whole prunes, and serve with a big bowl of mascarpone or crème fraîche.

COOKS' NOTE: Proceed with caution when making the syrup, as the Armagnac may ignite: this is normal—just the alcohol burning off. Leave it to continue to reduce.

ROULADE
with Provençal PEACHES

Update the classic jelly/jam Swiss roll into a ridiculously delicious dessert by adding your homemade bottled fruit. You can mix and match fruits and flavor creams, and freeze the roulade to serve it as a frozen dessert.

Preheat the oven to 375°F (190°C) Gas 5.

Whisk together the eggs and sugar for 5–6 minutes until pale and fluffy. Pour in the melted butter, add the salt, and stir to combine. Slowly fold in the flour and pour the batter onto the prepared baking sheet. Spread out evenly, and bake for 10–12 minutes, until golden and springy.

Remove from the oven and set aside for a few minutes. Sprinkle a clean dish towel/cloth with confectioners'/icing sugar. Invert the cake onto the towel and remove the parchment paper from the base. Beginning with the short sides, roll the cake up in the towel and leave to cool for 2 hours.

Place the reserved peach syrup in a small pan and bring to a boil until reduced by half.

Unroll the cake and remove the dish towel/cloth. Spread the crème fraîche evenly over the cake. Toss the sliced peaches and raspberries together in a bowl and place on top of the cake. Then roll it up tightly.

Place the cake seam-side down on a serving platter. Dust with confectioners'/icing sugar and serve with the warm syrup.

COOKS' NOTE: This recipe works well with any bottled fruits.

4 large eggs

½ cup/100 g golden granulated/caster sugar

2 tablespoons melted butter

½ teaspoon kosher/rock salt

1 cup/125 g cake/plain flour, sifted

confectioners'/icing sugar, for dusting

crème fraîche, to serve

6 Provençal Peaches (see page 77), drained with syrup reserved, and sliced

1½ cups/225 g fresh raspberries

a 13 x 9-inch/33 x 23-cm baking sheet, lined with baking parchment and lightly sprayed with vegetable oil

an electric stand mixer

SERVES 6–8

Indian-spiced APRICOTS

2 cups/400 g superfine/caster sugar
1 tablespoon cardamom pods, bashed
1 teaspoon ground cumin
½ teaspoon chili powder
¼ teaspoon allspice
1 cinnamon stick for each jar
24 apricots
still-warm sterilized glass jars with airtight lids

MAKES 4 CUPS (32 OZ.)/950 ML

I am crazy about Indian spices and use them at every opportunity. They give a wonderful balance of tart and sweet with a little heat. This is one of my favorite bottling spice recipes, it works well with any fruit.

Place the sugar and 4 cups (950 ml) water in a non-reactive pan and bring to a boil over medium–high heat. Cook for about 8 minutes until the sugar has dissolved. Remove from the heat and stir in the cardamom, cumin, chili, and allspice. Cover and set aside to cool for 15 minutes.

Place a cinnamon stick in each jar. Divide the apricots between warm, sterilized, glass jars, leaving a ¼-inch (5-mm) space at the top.

Strain the cooled syrup through a fine-mesh strainer/sieve, then pour it over the apricots. Carefully tap the jars on the counter top to get rid of air pockets. Wipe the jars clean and screw on the lids. Seal the jars for 25 minutes following the Oven Method or 15 minutes following the Water Bath Method (see page 9). Once sealed, store unopened in a cool, dark place for up to 12 months.

Star Anise KUMQUATS

1 cup/200 g superfine/caster sugar
60 firm kumquats
¼ cup/60 g crystallized ginger, roughly chopped
4 star anise pods
still-warm sterilized glass jars with airtight lids

MAKES 4 CUPS (32 OZ.)/950 ML

Kumquats can be a little on the tart side, so I include some crystalized ginger to add a little sweetness to the syrup. They're delicious in all kinds of Asian dishes and are a great pantry/store cupboard staple.

Place the sugar and 3 cups (700 ml) water in a non-reactive pan and bring to a boil. Reduce the heat and simmer for 8 minutes until the sugar has dissolved.

Pierce the kumquats with a small sharp knife. Layer them with the ginger in warm, sterilized, glass jars, leaving a ½-inch (1-cm) space at the top. Add 2 star anise to each jar. Pour the hot syrup over the kumquats and carefully tap the jars on the counter top to get rid of air pockets. Wipe the jars clean and screw on the lids. Seal the jars for 20 minutes following the Oven Method or 10 minutes following the Water Bath Method (see page 9). Once sealed, store unopened in a cool, dark place for up to 12 months.

Chai-infused PEARS

You can buy Chai tea bags to make this recipe even simpler, but the spices are found in most kitchens. It's fun to make your own mix and store it in a glass jar.

Begin by preparing the chai blend. Place the tea, cloves, allspice, cardamom, ginger, cinnamon, star anise, peppercorns, sugar, and 6 cups (1.4 litres) water in a non-reactive pan. Bring to a boil and reduce the heat. Simmer for 20 minutes, stirring occasionally. Remove the pan from the heat and set aside for 1 hour or overnight for a deeper flavor.

Strain the cooled chai through a fine mesh strainer/sieve and return to the pan. Bring to a boil, then reduce the heat to a simmer. Place the pears in the pan and gently cook for 10 minutes. Spoon the pears into sterilized glass jars, and pour over the hot syrup. Carefully tap the jars on the counter top to get rid of air pockets. Wipe the jars clean and screw on the lids. Seal the jars for 20 minutes following the Oven Method or 10 minutes following the Water Bath Method (see page 9). Once sealed, store unopened in a cool, dark place for up to 12 months.

2 black tea bags or 2 tablespoons of loose black tea

1 teaspoon cloves

½ teaspoon allspice

10 cardamom pods, bashed

1 teaspoon of ground ginger or crystallized ginger

½ teaspoon ground cinnamon

4 star anise

½ teaspoon whole black peppercorns

1½ cups/300 g cane sugar

6 firm pears, cut into wedges and core removed

sterilized glass jars with airtight lids

MAKES 8 CUPS (64 OZ.)/1.8 L

TANGERINES and Bay Leaves

Tangerines are great for making sorbet, ice cream, or any kind of dessert. Bay leaves add an earthiness to the fruit.

Peel the fruit over a bowl to catch all the juices, keeping the tangerines whole. Reserve the peel.

Place the sugar and 3 cups (700 ml) water in a non-reactive pan and bring to a boil over medium–high heat. Reduce the heat and simmer for about 8 minutes, until the sugar has dissolved. Add the orange blossom water and set aside.

Place the tangerines in warm, sterilized, glass jars, leaving a ½-inch (1-cm) space at the top. Place 2 bay leaves in each jar. Pour over the hot syrup and carefully tap the jars on the counter top to get rid of air pockets. Wipe the jars clean and screw on the lids. Seal the jars for 20 minutes following the Oven Method or 10 minutes following the Water Bath Method (see page 9). Once sealed, store unopened in a cool, dark place for up to 12 months.

16 small tangerines

1½ cups/300 g superfine/caster sugar

1 teaspoon orange blossom water

6 bay leaves

sterilized glass jars with airtight lids

MAKES 24 OZ./700 ML

RICOTTA TART
with Indian-spiced APRICOTS

PASTRY

2 cups/250 g all-purpose/plain flour

1½ sticks/175 g cold unsalted butter, cubed

pinch of sea salt

1 egg, lightly beaten

5 tablespoons iced water

FILLING

2 cups/450 g fresh ricotta

1 cup/225 g mascarpone

14 Indian-spiced Apricots (see page 84), drained
    with 1 cup/235 ml syrup reserved

a food processor

a 10-inch/25-cm tart pan, greased

baking beans

SERVES 6–8

This is a bit like an Eton mess dressed up in a tart shell. A swirl of spiced apricots in fresh ricotta and mascarpone drizzled with syrup makes for a lovely dessert any time of the year.

To make the pastry, place the flour, butter, and salt in a food processor and pulse until it resembles breadcrumbs. Add the egg and combine. With the motor running, add the iced water and process until the pastry comes together. Turn out onto a lightly floured surface and knead into a disc. Cover with plastic wrap/clingfilm and refrigerate for 30 minutes.

Remove the pastry from the refrigerator and roll out into a large circle on a lightly floured surface. Press into the prepared tart pan and trim the edges. Using a fork, prick the base of the tart all over. Cover with plastic wrap/clingfilm and return to the refrigerator for a further 30 minutes.

Preheat the oven to 375°F (190°C) Gas 5.

Remove the pastry from the refrigerator and line the bottom with a circle of parchment paper. Top with baking beans and bake for 20 minutes. Remove the paper and beans and bake for another 20 minutes until the shell is golden. Remove from the oven and set aside to cool completely.

Place the ricotta and mascarpone in a bowl and whisk together. Tear the apricots in half, add to the bowl, and mix thoroughly. Spoon the mascarpone mix into the cooled tart shell and spread out to the edges.

Drizzle with a little spiced syrup and serve the rest alongside in a small pitcher/jug.

Buckwheat
PANCAKES
with Chai-infused PEARS

I love the nuttiness of buckwheat pancakes. Topped with amazing syrupy pears infused with chai spices, it just doesn't get any better. I like to make these for brunch, but I have been known to do a version for dessert—it's the perfect comfort food.

Place the flour, sugar, baking powder, and salt in a bowl and mix together. In a separate bowl, whisk together the milk, vanilla, butter, and egg. Pour the milk mixture into the flour mixture and whisk until just combined.

Heat a skillet/frying pan over medium–high heat and drizzle with a little vegetable oil. Using a ¼-cup (60 ml) measuring cup, pour cups of batter two at a time into the pan. When bubbles start appearing on the top of the pancakes, flip them over and press down gently on the tops with the back of the spatula. Cook for 2–3 minutes, until golden brown and cooked through. Transfer to a warm plate and cover with a clean dish towel/cloth to keep warm.

Heat the pears and their syrup in a small pan over medium heat.

To serve, place a stack of pancakes on each plate and top with spoonfuls of the warm pears and the syrup.

1½ cups/200 g buckwheat flour
¼ cup/50 g maple sugar or light brown sugar
2 teaspoons baking powder
a pinch of kosher/rock salt
1½ cups/350 ml milk
1 teaspoon vanilla extract
2 tablespoons melted butter
1 egg
vegetable oil, for frying
Chai-infused Pears (see page 85)

a ¼-cup/60-ml measuring cup
SERVES 4

Amaretto CHERRIES

½ cup/100 g sugar

½ cup/170 g honey

⅓ cup/80 ml Amaretto or other almond liqueur

6 cups/900 g dark red cherries , rinsed and pit/stones removed

still-warm sterilized glass jars with airtight lids

MAKES 4½ CUPS (36 OZ.)/1 L

As soon as cherry season arrives, go along and buy as many as you can. Cherries are the perfect little fruit to bottle, pickle, jam or make into spoon fruit.

Combine the sugar, honey, Amaretto and 3 cups (700 ml) water in a non-reactive pan and bring to a boil over medium–high heat. Cook for about 8 minutes, until the sugar has dissolved. Reduce the heat and add the rinsed and pitted/stoned cherries. Simmer for 5 minutes, until the cherries plump up and are lightly cooked. Turn off the heat and let the cherries rest in the syrup for 5 minutes.

Pour the cherries and syrup into warm, sterilized, glass jars, leaving a ¼-inch (5-mm) space at the top. Carefully tap the jars on the counter top to get rid of air pockets. Wipe the jars clean and screw on the lids. Seal the jars for 20 minutes following the Oven Method or 10 minutes following the Water Bath Method (see page 9). Once sealed, store unopened in a cool, dark place for up to 12 months.

Rhubarb & GINGER

Rhubarb is one of the best flavors in the world, but those tough, sour stalks need some love before bottling them. It only takes a few minutes to cook them in a sugar and ginger water, and they are ready to use.

Begin by preparing the rhubarb. Trim the ends and cut the stalks into 1-inch (2.5-cm) pieces. In a non-reactive pan over medium–high heat, dissolve the sugar and honey in 2 cups (475 ml) water. Add the rhubarb and ginger and bring to a boil. Reduce the heat and continue to cook for a further 5 minutes.

Pour the rhubarb into warm, sterilized, glass jars and carefully tap the jars on the counter top to get rid of air pockets. Wipe the jars clean and screw on the lids. Seal the jars for 20 minutes following the Oven Method or 10 minutes following the Water Bath Method (see page 9). Once sealed, store unopened in a cool, dark place for up to 12 months.

6 ½ cups/675 g chopped fresh rhubarb
¾ cup/150 g white sugar
½ cup/170 g honey
2 tablespoons finely chopped crystallized ginger
still-warm sterilized glass jars with airtight lids

MAKES 4 CUPS (32 OZ.)/950 ML

CLEMENTINES with Kaffir Lime Leaves

There is a great bonus to bottling clementines: the peel. Dry the peels at a low temperature in the oven until completely dry. When cooled, grind in a spice mill or coffee grinder, and add the powder to sugar or salt. You can also candy the peel and store it for baking.

Peel the fruit over a bowl to catch all the juices, keeping the clementines whole. Reserve the peel.

Place the sugar and 3 cups (700 ml) water in a non-reactive pan and bring to a boil over medium–high heat. Reduce the heat and simmer for about 8 minutes, until the sugar has dissolved.

Pack the clementines into warm, sterilized, glass jars, leaving a ½-inch (1-cm) space at the top. Place 2–3 lime leaves in each jar. Pour over the hot syrup and carefully tap the jars on the counter top to get rid of air pockets. Wipe the jars clean and screw on the lids. Seal the jars for 25 minutes following the Oven Method or 15 minutes following the Water Bath Method (see page 9). Once sealed, store unopened in a cool, dark place for up to 12 months.

1 cup/200 g superfine/caster sugar
24 small clementines
4–6 kaffir lime leaves
still-warm sterilized glass jars with airtight lids

MAKES 8 CUPS (64 OZ.)/1.8 L

Lemon Curd
TARTLETS
with Rhubarb & GINGER

1 quantity Pastry (see page 86)

LEMON CURD

5 eggs

¾ cup/150 g fine white sugar

grated zest and juice of 3 large lemons or
    ½ cup/125 ml lemon juice

1½ sticks/175 g unsalted butter, cubed and
    room temperature

TO SERVE

Rhubarb & Ginger (see page 91)

edible flowers

a food processor

10 x 3-inch (7.5-cm) tartlet pans, greased and
    floured

baking parchment

baking beans

MAKES 10

Lemon curd is one of the easiest things to make, and can form the base of soufflés, ice creams, and fillers for cakes and tarts. The bright citrus gives vibrancy to this tart and enhances the delicious rhubarb and ginger.

Preheat the oven to 350°F (180°C) Gas 4.

After the pastry has rested in the refrigerator for 30 minutes, roll it out onto a lightly floured surface into a large circle. Cut it into circles big enough to line the tart pans. Press the pastry circles into the pans, trim the edges and prick the bases with a fork. Cover with plastic wrap/clingfilm and chill for another 30 minutes.

To make the lemon curd, place the eggs, sugar, lemon zest, and juice in a heatproof bowl set over a pan one-third filled with water. Bring to a boil over medium–high heat, then reduce to a simmer. Whisk for about 8 minutes until the sugar has dissolved and the mixture has thickened. Add the cubes of butter one at a time and whisk until smooth, then remove from the heat. Set aside to cool.

Remove the tartlets from the refrigerator, line with baking parchment, and top with baking beans. Bake in the oven for 5 minutes, then remove the paper and weights. Return to the oven and bake for a further 8–10 minutes, until golden. Remove from the oven and cool on a wire rack.

To assemble, fill the tartlet shells with lemon curd, then top with a generous teaspoon of Rhubarb & Ginger. Sprinkle with edible flowers and serve.

COOKS' NOTE: Leftover lemon curd will keep in the refrigerator for 10 days. It is delicious spread it on toast for breakfast.

Jam Jar
CRUMBLES
with Amaretto CHERRIES

Baking crumbles in jam jars has to be the best-kept secret around. Genius for outdoor entertaining and transporting to picnics, it is also a nostalgic nod to childhood, when everything seemed to be served in glass jars.

Preheat the oven to 375°F (190°C) Gas 5.

To make the crumble, place the flour, butter, and sugar in a food processor and pulse until the mixture resembles breadcrumbs. Stir in the granola and almonds and set aside.

Spoon the Amaretto Cherries equally between the glass jars and push the fruit down. Generously top the jars with the crumble and bake in the oven for 20 minutes, until the topping is golden-brown and crispy.

Remove from the oven and serve with a big bowl of mascarpone or vanilla ice cream.

COOKS' NOTE: If there is a little crumble topping left over, it can be stored in the freezer for another time.

¼ cup/30 g all-purpose/plain flour
½ stick/60 g butter
2 tablespoons brown sugar
¼ cup/30 g granola
2 tablespoons almond meal/ground almonds
4 cups/950 ml Amaretto Cherries (see page 90)
mascarpone or vanilla ice cream, to serve

4 x 1-cup/250-ml glass jars

SERVES 4

SPOON FRUIT, CANDIES & PASTES

Spoon Fruits are found all over Greece. They are preserved in a wonderfully thick, gooey, sweet syrup, and get their name from the way they are traditionally served on a spoon, accompanied with an icy cold glass of water. It's a very welcoming way to recover from the heat of the sun.

Stone fruits in syrup such a Vin Santo Plum Spoon Fruit (page 98) are delicious to eat alone or with a piece of cheese. Dress up an everyday Frangipane Tart (page 102) with a few whole fruits, drizzle with the thick, heavenly syrup, and serve with lashings of cream. Figs are the classic fruit to preserve in this way and can be used in all kinds of baking. Serve them as a condiment alongside roasted game or simply adorn a wonderful light and creamy Yogurt Panna Cotta (page 105) with one.

Embellish the syrups with wonderful liqueurs, brandies, herbs, scented flowers and perfumed waters. They all add a wonderfully light floral layer to the preserves. I store leftover syrup in the refrigerator and add to homemade cordials poured over shaved ice. They can also be drizzled over fresh cheeses, such as ricotta, labneh, and ice cream. And of course, they can be poured into a tall, iced glass, and topped up with cold Prosecco for a lovely, fizzy cocktail.

Citrus fruits compliment the sweetness of the sugar syrup. Bake a batch of Orange Rosemary Cakes (page 108) and top with Blood Orange Spoon Fruit (page 107), serve warm with a pot of coffee, and relax. Citrus is a gift deep in the dark and lacklustre winter months. The farmers' market glows with an abundance of oranges, lemons, limes and grapefruits in all their glory. Freshly picked citrus peels, dried in sugar, can be used in an array of baking recipes, and especially so for decorating. Flavor ice creams with them and enjoy such delights as Tutti Frutti Semifreddo (page 119). Not a piece of the fruit goes to waste—juice the flesh and enjoy sipping it while you are preparing the candied peel. The key to peeling the skin is a razor-sharp peeler so you don't end up with any pith.

Source very ripe fruit to make the pastes as it's all about taste and not the look in these recipes. End an extraordinary meal with any of the pastes in this chapter. Serve them alongside a robust cheeseboard and pour a good homemade liqueur to wash it all down with. Spread lavishly on warm, thick-cut slices of bread and on charred grilled meats for a wonderful glaze; or spoon a little into a hot pan to deglaze pan-fried chicken.

Pastes work well if they are set in small amounts or you may have different shaped containers that you want to store them in. Decide on the size and number of jars you want to use or have to hand at the time. Spoon Fruits are very sweet so I like to store mine in small glass jars, only using a little at a time, therefore preventing waste or spoilage once opened. The size of fruit differs each time so it's a good idea to decide before you begin whether you want to keep the fruit whole or cut. Measure the fruit in the jars you wish to use before you begin.

Sauternes APRICOT SPOON FRUIT

30 firm apricots, rinsed and pits/stones removed

¼ cup/50 g granulated/caster sugar

12 oz./375 ml Sauternes or other dessert wine

4 flowering thyme sprigs

½ vanilla bean/pod per jar, cut lengthwise

still-warm sterilized glass jars with airtight lids

MAKES 4 CUPS (32 OZ.)/950 ML

Blenheims are my favorite apricot as they are small, rosy and very sweet. The thyme adds a floral note to the syrup.

Pour the Sauternes into a non-reactive pan and add the sugar. Bring to a boil over a medium–high heat. Reduce the heat and simmer for about 5 minutes, stirring occasionally until the sugar is completely dissolved.

Add the apricots to the pan and cook for 2 minutes. Remove the apricots with a slotted spoon and pack into warm, sterilized, glass jars, leaving a ¼-inch (5-mm) space at the top. Divide the flowering thyme sprigs and vanilla between the jars.

Bring the Sauternes syrup back to a boil and continue to cook for a further few minutes until it has thickened and reduced a little.

Pour the hot syrup over the fruit and carefully tap the jars on the counter top to get rid of air pockets. Wipe the jars clean and screw on the lids. Seal the jars for 20 minutes following the Oven Method or 10 minutes following the Water Bath Method (see page 9). Once sealed, store unopened in a cool, dark place for up to 12 months.

Vin Santo PLUM SPOON FRUIT

16 firm plums, rinsed

1½ cups/350 ml Vin Santo or other dessert wine

2 tablespoons freshly squeezed lemon juice

1½ cups/275 g granulated/caster sugar

6 thyme sprigs

still-warm sterilized glass jars with airtight lids

MAKES 4 CUPS (32 OZ.)/950 ML

I use Santa Rosa plums here, which are a delicious and very juicy, deep red plum.

Pour the Vin Santo and lemon juice into a non-reactive pan over a medium–high heat, and add the sugar. Bring to a boil, then reduce the heat and simmer for 6–8 minutes, until the sugar is completely dissolved.

Add the plums to the pan and cook for 3 minutes. Remove the plums with a slotted spoon and pack into warm, sterilized, glass jars, leaving a ¼-inch (5-mm) space at the top. Divide the thyme between the jars.

Bring the Vin Santo syrup to a boil and continue to cook for a further few minutes until it has thickened and reduced a little. Pour the hot syrup over the fruit and carefully tap the jars on the counter top to get rid of air pockets. Wipe the jars clean and screw on the lids. Seal the jars for 20 minutes following the Oven Method or 10 minutes following the Water Bath Method (see page 9). Once sealed, store unopened in a cool, dark place for up to 12 months.

Fig SPOON FRUIT

In Greece, figs are stuffed with nuts before preserving, and the syrup served over ice to make a refreshing drink.

In a non-reactive pan bring the sugar and 1 cup (235 ml) of water to a boil over a medium–high heat. Reduce the heat and simmer for 10 minutes, stirring occasionally until the sugar is completely dissolved. Remove the pan from the heat and add the port. Stir, then return the pan to the heat, and cook for a further 2 minutes. Carefully add the figs, swirl the pan to coat the figs, and simmer for 10 minutes. Remove the pan from the heat and let the figs rest in the syrup for a further 10 minutes.

Spoon the figs and syrup into warm, sterilized, glass jars leaving a ¼-inch (5-mm) space at the top. Carefully tap the jars on the counter top to get rid of air pockets. Wipe the jars clean and screw on the lids. Seal the jars for 20 minutes following the Oven Method or 10 minutes following the Water Bath Method (see page 9). Once sealed, store unopened in a cool, dark place for up to 12 months.

12 firm figs, rinsed
1 cup/200 g granulated/caster sugar
2 tablespoons port

still-warm sterilized glass jars with airtight lids

MAKES 2 CUPS (16 OZ.)/475 ML

Cherry & Rose Geranium SPOON FRUIT

I have two pots of Rose Geranium that sit proudly by my kitchen door. I use the leaves to perfume creams, jams and desserts, and the pretty pink flowers as décor.

In a non-reactive pan bring the sugar and ½ cup (120 ml) of water to a boil over a medium–high heat. Reduce the heat and simmer for 8 minutes, stirring occasionally until the sugar is completely dissolved. Add the cherries, gently stir, and simmer for 2 minutes. Remove the cherries with a slotted spoon, carefully shaking any excess syrup back into the pan.

Spoon the cherries into warm, sterilized, glass jars leaving ¼-inch (5-mm) space at the top. Rub the geranium leaves between your fingers to release the oils then add them to the pan with the syrup. Add the lemon juice and bring to the boil. Continue to cook for about 10 minutes until the syrup becomes thick and reduces slightly. Remove from the heat and take out the geranium leaves.

Pour the hot syrup over the cherries and carefully tap the jars on the counter top to get rid of air pockets. Wipe the jars clean and screw on the lids. Seal the jars following the method above and on page 9. Once sealed, store unopened in a cool, dark place for up to 12 months.

3 ⅓ cups/450 g firm cherries, rinsed and pits/stones removed
1 cup/200 g granulated/caster sugar
1 tablespoon freshly squeezed lemon juice
the sprigs and flowers of 1 rose geranium

still-warm sterilized glass jars with airtight lids

MAKES 2 CUPS (16 OZ.)/475 ML

Frangipane
TART
with Vin Santo PLUMS

1 quantity Pastry (see page 86)
1 cup/100 g finely ground almonds
1 stick/115 g butter
½ cup/100 g superfine/caster sugar
2 eggs, lightly beaten
2 tablespoons all-purpose/plain flour
2 teaspoons baking powder
¼ teaspoon pure vanilla extract
1 tablespoon Amaretto or other almond liqueur
Vin Santo Plums (see page 98), stoned

a food processor
2 rectangular tart pans or a 10-inch/ 25-cm
    round tart pan, greased
an electric stand mixer

SERVES 6–8

Frangipane is a complete crowd-pleaser for any occasion. Toasting the almonds gives the tart a nutty, rich flavor. Sometimes I make it in a rectangular pan (as pictured) and other times round either way it's always great.

Once the pastry has rested in the refrigerator for 30 minutes, roll it out on to a lightly floured surface into a large rectangle. Press the pastry into the prepared tart pan and trim the edges. Using a fork prick the base of the tart all over. Cover with plastic wrap/clingfilm and return to the refrigerator for 30 minutes.

Preheat the oven to 350°F (175°C) Gas 4.

Toast the ground almonds over a medium heat until golden and set aside.

In an electric stand mixer cream together the butter and sugar until light and fluffy. Slowly add the eggs and beat until combined. Add the flour, baking powder, pure vanilla extract, and Amaretto, and continue to beat until completely mixed. Stir in the ground almonds.

Pour the frangipane mixture into the pastry shell and top with Vin Santo plums—as many as you want. Bake in the preheated oven for 45 minutes, until the mixture has risen, and is golden and firm to the touch. It will puff up while cooking but then sinks a little when cooling. Remove from the oven and cool for 10 minutes.

In a small pan heat the Vin Santo Plum syrup. Drizzle the warm syrup over the tart and serve.

COOKS' NOTE: You can make this tart in a round or 2 rectangular tart pans as well as making individual tarts.

Yogurt
PANNA COTTA
with Fig SPOON FRUIT

This is one of my all-time favorite deserts—it's so simple and delicate. Adorned with plump fig spoon fruits it is a feast for the eyes. It works really well as a dessert for a weekend get-together as you can make it up to 2 days ahead and then relax.

First, dissolve the gelatin with a tablespoon of warm water.

Combine the cream, milk, sugar, and vanilla seeds in a small saucepan over a medium heat, and bring to the boil. Reduce the heat and stirring constantly cook until the sugar has dissolved about 5 minutes. Remove from the heat and add the gelatin. Whisk until completely incorporated and set aside to cool.

Place the yogurt and lemon zest in a bowl and whisk together. Gradually pour in the cooled cream mixture, and continue to whisk until smooth. Pour the mixture into the ramekins and cover. Place in the refrigerator to set.

To serve, turn out each panna cotta onto a small serving plate. Top with a Fig Spoon Fruit and a drizzle of syrup.

COOKS' NOTE: You can also leave and serve the panna cotta in the bowls they set in—just top with figs and syrup.

2 teaspoons gelatin powder
1 cup/235 ml heavy/double cream
1½ cups/355 ml whole milk
¼ cup/50 g superfine/caster sugar
1 vanilla bean/pod, halved and seeds removed
2 cups/430 g natural set yogurt
2 teaspoons grated lemon zest
Fig Spoon Fruit (see page 101), to serve

8 x ¾ cup/180 ml ramekins
SERVES 8

Rioja & Allspice PEARS

8 firm pears, cored and cut into quarters
3 cups/750 ml Rioja
1 cup/200 g brown sugar
1 tablespoon allspice
grated zest of 1 orange

still-warm sterilized glass jars with airtight lids

MAKES 8 CUPS (64 OZ.)/1.8 L

I love the dark intense color the Rioja gives to these pears but this Spanish red wine also gives the syrup a robust and pleasing taste. Allspice brings all of the flavors together. I like to use these pears for tarts and galettes. They are also a spectacular addition to any cheese plate.

Pour the Rioja into a non-reactive pan and add the sugar, allspice, and orange zest. Bring to a boil over a medium–high heat. Reduce the heat and simmer for 10 minutes, stirring occasionally until the sugar is completely dissolved. Add the pears to the pan and gently cook for 5 minutes. Remove the pears with a slotted spoon and pack into warm, sterilized, glass jars, leaving a ¼-inch (5-mm) space at the top.

Pour the hot Rioja syrup over the fruit and carefully tap the jars on the counter top to get rid of air pockets. Wipe the jars clean and screw on the lids. Seal the jars for 20 minutes following the Oven Method or 10 minutes following the Water Bath Method (see page 9). Once sealed, store unopened in a cool, dark place for up to 12 months.

Blood Orange SPOON FRUIT

These dark ruby jewels make beautiful spoon fruits, which can be used in all sorts of ways.

Place the sugar, honey, and water in a non-reactive pan and bring to a boil over a medium–high heat. Reduce the heat and simmer for 8 minutes, stirring occasionally until the sugar is completely dissolved. Add the orange slices and cook for 2–3 minutes.

Remove the oranges with a slotted spoon and carefully shake off any excess syrup back into the pan. Arrange the orange slices into warm, sterilized, glass jars, leaving a ¼-inch (5-mm) space at the top. Return the pan to the heat and bring the syrup to a boil. Continue to cook for about 20 minutes, until the syrup has reduced and thickened. Pour the hot syrup over the fruit and carefully tap the jars on the counter top to get rid of air pockets. Wipe the jars clean and screw on the lids. Seal the jars for 20 minutes following the Oven Method or 10 minutes following the Water Bath Method (see page 9). Once sealed, store unopened in a cool, dark place for up to 12 months.

6 blood oranges, cut into ¼-inch/5-mm rounds, pips removed

1 cup/200 g granulated/caster sugar

1 cup/340 g clear honey

3 cups/700 ml water

still-warm sterilized glass jars with airtight lids

MAKES 8 CUPS (64 OZ.)/1.8 L

Lemon & Lime SPOON FRUIT

Use this bitter and tangy spoon fruit chopped up in salsa, marinades and desserts. The juice is exceptionally good for cocktails or a dash added to an ice-cold glass of Prosecco.

Layer the bottom of a non-reactive pan with the prepared citrus fruit slices. Reserve ½ cup (100 g) of the sugar to use later. Sprinkle over a little of the remaining sugar and continue to layer the fruit and sugar in this way, finishing with sugar. Add the cardamom pods and cover with about 3 cups (700 ml) of cold water, making sure the fruit is submerged. Place a piece of baking parchment on top and partially cover with a lid. Bring to the boil, lower the heat and gently simmer for about 2½ hours. Remove the fruit with a slotted spoon, carefully shaking any excess syrup back into the pan.

Spoon the fruit into warm, sterilized, glass jars leaving ¼-inch (5-mm) space at the top. Add the reserved sugar to the pan and bring to the boil. Cook until the syrup is thick and reduced by half. Pour over the fruit and tap the jars on the counter top to get rid of any air pockets. Wipe the jars clean and screw on the lids. Seal the jars as instructed in the recipe above. Once sealed, store unopened in a cool, dark place for up to 12 months.

6 lemons and 2 limes, rinsed and cut into ½-inch/1-cm rounds, pips removed as you go

3 cups/600 g granulated/caster sugar, plus extra for sprinkling

4 cardamom pods, bruised

still-warm sterilized glass jars with airtight lids

MAKES 8 CUPS (64 OZ.)/1.8 L

Orange
ROSEMARY CAKES
with Blood Orange SPOON FRUIT

2 sticks/230 g unsalted butter

¾ cup/150 g cane sugar

3 large/medium eggs

½ cup/65 g almond meal/flour

1½ cups/150 g all-purpose/plain flour

½ teaspoon baking powder

½ teaspoon baking soda/bicarbonate of soda

½ teaspoon salt

12 sprigs fresh rosemary, finely chopped

grated zest of 1 lemon

6 slices Blood Orange Spoon Fruit (see page 107), halved, plus syrup to serve

an electric stand mixer

a muffin pan, lightly greased

MAKES 12

You can eat these cakes straight from the pan and enjoy with coffee or serve up as dessert with a large scoop of ice cream. They make great food for the beach or picnic as they are easy to pack up and travel well.

Preheat the oven to 350°F (175°C) Gas 4.

In an electric stand mixer cream together the butter and sugar on a medium–high speed until light and fluffy. Reduce the speed, add the eggs one at a time, and beat until smooth.

Add the flour and almond meal a little at a time until well combined, scraping down the sides as necessary. Add the baking powder, baking soda/bicarbonate of soda, salt, rosemary, and lemon zest, and continue to mix until fully incorporated.

Spoon the mixture into the prepared muffin pan and top each cake with a piece of Blood Orange Spoon Fruit. Place a sprig of rosemary on top and bake in the preheated oven for 18–20 minutes until golden brown and cooked through.

Remove from the oven and drizzle each cake with the syrup from the jar of blood oranges. Serve immediately.

Orange Blossom
SHREDDED SPOON FRUIT

6 firm Valencia oranges

1½ cups/275 g granulated/caster sugar

freshly squeezed juice of 1 orange

1 teaspoon orange flower water

1 tablespoon Cointreau or other orange liqueur

1 tablespoon of orange blossom honey

still-warm sterilized glass jars with airtight lids

an oil-resistant thermometer

MAKES 4 CUPS (32 OZ.)/950 ML

Use large ripe oranges with thick skins. Spoon fruits are preserved in thick sugary syrups. I like to preserve mine in small jars so I can use a little at a time. This is a great way to use up peel when juicing oranges.

Peel the oranges into strips making sure you get no pith on the peel. Cut the peels into thin matchsticks and set aside.

Bring a pan of water to the boil and drop in the orange matchsticks and simmer for 25 minutes. This will get rid of any bitterness.

Drain the orange strips in a colander and set aside. Return the empty pan to a medium–high heat and add the sugar and orange juice. Bring to a boil then reduce the heat and simmer for 10 minutes, stirring occasionally until the sugar has completely dissolved. Add the reserved orange strips and cook for a further 10 minutes.

Remove the orange strips with a slotted spoon gently shaking any excess syrup back into the pan and set aside. Add the orange water and Cointreau to the pan and bring the syrup back to a boil. Continue to cook for about 8 minutes until it becomes thick and has reduced slightly. The syrup must read 240°F (115°C) on a thermometer. Remove the pan from the heat, add the reserved orange strips, and rest for 5 minutes.

Pack the oranges and syrup into warm, sterilized, glass jars, leaving a ¼-inch (5-mm) space at the top. Carefully tap the jars on the counter top to get rid of air pockets. Wipe the jars clean and screw on the lids. Seal the jars for 15 minutes following the Oven Method or 10 minutes following the Water Bath Method (see page 9). Once sealed, store unopened in a cool, dark place for up to 12 months.

COOKS' NOTE: Make sure your peeler is razor sharp or you will end up with a lot of bitter pith attached to your shredded spoon fruit.

Nectarine & Serrano PASTE

I am a fan of sweet and spicy pairings. If you have a lower tolerance for spice, and depending on how hot the Serranos are, then simply decrease the quantity used here. Don't leave them out as they give a wonderful kick to the sweet nectarines.

Place the nectarine quarters in a preserving pan or large saucepan and add 1 cup (275 ml) of water. Bring to the boil over a medium–high heat. Reduce the heat and simmer for about 20 minutes, stirring occasionally until the nectarines are soft and broken down.

Place the nectarines in a blender and purée. Return the purée to the pan and add the serranos, sugar, and lemon juice. Bring to a boil, reduce the heat, and simmer for 45 minutes, stirring frequently.

Spoon the paste into warm, sterilized, glass jars leaving a ¼-inch (5-mm) space from the top. Carefully tap them on the counter top to get rid of air pockets. Wipe the jars clean and screw on the lids. Seal the jars for 20 minutes following the Oven Method or 10 minutes following the Water Bath Method (see page 9). Once sealed, store unopened in a cool, dark place for up to 12 months.

16 ripe nectarines, pits/stones removed and cut into quarters

2 Serrano peppers, thinly sliced with seeds included

4½ cups/900 g granulated/caster sugar

freshly squeezed juice of 1 lemon

sterilized glass jars with airtight lids

MAKES 4 CUPS (32 OZ.)/950 ML

Apple Sage & Calvados PASTE

6 apples, peeled, core removed, and diced

½ cup/125 ml Calvados or other apple liqueur

2¼ cups/450 g granulated/caster sugar

1 teaspoon dried sage

grated zest and freshly squeezed juice of 1 lemon

sterilized glass jars with airtight lids

MAKES 4 CUPS (32 OZ.)/950 ML

Quinces can be hard to come by so I have adapted the famous Spanish Membrillo recipe by using apples instead.

Place the apple pieces in a large pan with 3 cups (700 ml) of cold water. Bring to the boil over a medium–high heat. Reduce the heat and simmer for about 45 minutes, stirring occasionally, until the apples are soft.

Place the cooked apples in a blender and purée. Return the purée to the pan and add the Calvados, sugar, sage, lemon zest and juice. Bring to the boil, reduce the heat, and simmer for about 40 minutes, stirring frequently. The paste should be thick and deep in color.

Spoon the paste into warm, sterilized, glass jars leaving a ¼-inch (5-mm) space from the top. Carefully tap them on the counter top to get rid of air pockets. Wipe the jars clean and screw on the lids. Seal the jars for 20 minutes following the Oven Method or 10 minutes following the Water Bath Method (see page 9). Once sealed, store unopened in a cool, dark place for up to 12 months.

Peach & Pistachio PASTE

12 ripe peaches, pits/stones removed and cut into quarters

1 cup/250 ml water

3⅓ cups/650 g brown sugar

1 cup/120 g ground pistachios

sterilized glass jars with airtight lids

MAKES 4 CUPS (32 OZ.)/950 ML

Making pastes is really easy—it's like making jam. This is where the fun begins as you can use flavored sugars and really go wild with different fruits and nuts.

Place the peach quarters in a large pan with 1 cup (235 ml) of water. Bring to the boil over a medium–high heat. Reduce the heat and simmer for about 20 minutes, stirring occasionally, until the peaches are soft.

Place the cooked peaches in a blender and purée. Return the purée to the pan and add the sugar. Bring to the boil, reduce the heat, and simmer for about 45 minutes, stirring frequently. Add the pistachios and cook for a further 5 minutes.

Spoon the paste into warm, sterilized, glass jars leaving a ¼-inch (5-mm) space from the top. Carefully tap them on the counter top to get rid of air pockets. Wipe the jars clean and screw on the lids. Seal the jars for 20 minutes following the Oven Method or 10 minutes following the Water Bath Method (see page 9). Once sealed, store unopened in a cool, dark place for up to 12 months.

Plum & Bay PASTE

The dark ruby color of this paste makes it the center of attention. Bay leaves add a rich, herbal flavor to the sweet plums. This paste is fantastic not only with cheeses but grilled meats and chicken.

Rinse the plums and cut them in half. Remove the stones. Place them in a large pan and add 1 cup (250 ml) of water and the bay leaves. Bring to the boil over a medium–high heat. Reduce the heat and simmer for about 20 minutes, stirring occasionally, until the plums are soft.

Place the cooked plums in a blender and purée. Return the purée to the pan and add the Madeira, sugar, and lemon juice. Bring to the boil, reduce the heat, and simmer, for about 30 minutes, stirring frequently.

Spoon the paste into warm, sterilized, glass jars leaving a ¼-inch (5-mm) space from the top. Carefully tap them on the counter top to get rid of air pockets. Wipe the jars clean and screw on the lids. Seal the jars for 20 minutes following the Oven Method or 10 minutes following the Water Bath Method (see page 9). Once sealed, store unopened in a cool, dark place for up to 12 months.

COOKS' NOTE: The paste can be poured into lightly oiled cake pans, then cut into small squares, and rolled lightly in sugar coconut or nuts to make delicious fruit candies.

24 ripe plums, cut in half, pits/stones removed
2 bay leaves
2 tablespoons Madeira wine
4 ½ cups/900 g granulated/caster sugar
freshly squeezed juice of 1 lemon

sterilized glass jars with airtight lids

MAKES 4 CUPS (32 OZ.)/950 ML

Taleggio
TOASTS
with Plum & Bay PASTE

Taleggio is a creamy mild Italian cheese that is used in salads and risottos. It is perfect for grilling as it melts easily. Match it with any of the fruit pastes and you won't be disappointed.

Preheat the broiler/grill to high. Place the bread on a baking sheet and brush each side with olive oil. Grill them under the pre-heated broiler/grill on both sides until golden.

Remove the toast from the broiler/grill and place a piece of taleggio cheese on top of each, making sure to cover the surface. Place a slice of Plum & Bay Paste on top of the cheese and sprinkle with a few fresh thyme leaves.

Return the toasts to the broiler/grill and grill until the cheese and paste is golden and melted. Serve immediately.

9 thick slices bread
olive oil, to brush
1 lb./500 g taleggio cheese, sliced
1 small bunch fresh thyme
Plum & Bay Paste (see page 113)

a baking sheet

SERVES 8

Candied CITRUS

6 lemons or 4 oranges or 8 limes

3½ cups/700 g superfine/caster sugar

a baking sheet, sprinkled with superfine/
caster sugar

MAKES 2 CUPS (16 OZ.)/475 ML

If there is one thing that should be homemade it's candied peel. The store-bought variety just sits around and has no flavor or aroma. This may seem a little laborious but it reaps huge rewards and you will never look at candied citrus in the same way again. You can juice the oranges once peeled and refrigerate for later.

Peel the oranges into strips making sure you get no pith on the peel. Cut the peels into thin matchsticks and set aside.

Bring a small pan of water to the boil and drop the peel into it. Cook for 10 minutes. Drain the peel and repeat the process. This will get rid of any bitterness in the peel.

Bring the sugar and 3 cups (700 ml) of water to a boil over a medium–high heat. Reduce the heat and simmer for 5 minutes, stirring occasionally, until the sugar has completely dissolved. Add the peel and bring to a boil, then reduce the heat to a rapid simmer. Continue to cook for another 20 minutes brushing down the sides with a pastry brush as necessary. Turn off the heat and allow the citrus to cool in the syrup for at least 1 hour.

Preheat the oven to 250°F (120°C) Gas ½.

Remove the peel from the pan with a slotted spoon, shaking any excess syrup back into the pan. Toss the peel in the sugar on the prepared baking sheet and bake in the preheated oven for 45 minutes. Remove form the oven and allow to cool before serving. Store in airtight containers for up to 6 months.

COOKS' NOTE: Reserve the excess syrup for baking, pouring over ice cream and pancakes, making sorbets, cocktails, desserts, and marinades.

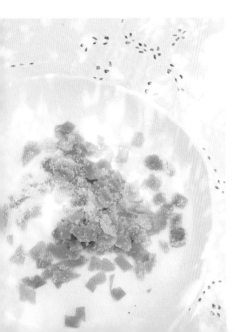

Candied LIME & COCONUT
BISCOTTI

I fell in love with biscotti in my home town in Scotland where there were several Italian coffee shops and ice cream parlors. This is my tropical version, which I serve with homemade coconut ice cream.

Preheat the oven to 325°F (160°C) Gas 3.

Cream together the butter and sugar in a electric stand mixer until light and fluffy. Add the eggs, one at a time, and beat until the mixture is smooth. Add the lemon extract and slowly add in the flour, baking powder, and salt, and continue to beat until completely mixed. Stir in the candied peel, coconut, and pistachios.

Turn the dough out onto a lightly floured surface and divide in two. Roll the dough into a log shapes, approximately 10-inches (25-cm) long by 2½-inches (6.5-cm) thick. Pat down the top to gently flatten. Place the two logs on one of the prepared baking sheets making sure there is a 2-inch (5-cm) gap between them as they spread a little. Bake in the preheated oven for 20–25 minutes until lightly golden. Remove from the oven and cool for 10 minutes.

Turn the oven down to 300°F (150°C) Gas 2.

Using a sharp knife, gently cut the biscotti at an angle into ½-inch (10-mm) pieces. Lay on the remaining baking sheets and cook for 6–8 minutes on each side until golden. Remove from the oven and place on a cooling rack.

Drizzle with melted white chocolate and leave to set before serving. When completely cool store in airtight containers.

COOKS' NOTE: To make smaller biscotti, divide the dough into four, and roll into smaller logs, approximately 8-inches (20-cm) long by 1½-inches (4-cm) thick.

1 stick/115 g unsalted butter
½ cup/110 g light brown sugar
2 US large/UK medium eggs
½ teaspoon lemon extract or lemongrass extract
2 cups/250 g all-purpose/plain flour
1¼ teaspoons baking powder
½ teaspoon salt
3 tablespoons Candied Lime Peel (see previous page)
½ cup/35 g shredded unsweetened coconut
½ cup/60 g ground pistachios
white chocolate, melted (optional)

an electric stand mixer
3–4 baking sheet lined with baking parchment

MAKES 36

Tutti Frutti
SEMIFREDDO
with Candied CITRUS

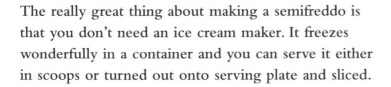

The really great thing about making a semifreddo is that you don't need an ice cream maker. It freezes wonderfully in a container and you can serve it either in scoops or turned out onto serving plate and sliced.

Combine the eggs, yolks, and sugar in a heatproof bowl and place over a pot of simmering water. Whisk the mixture with an electric hand whisk on a high speed for about 5 minutes, until it turns into pale yellow ribbons and has thickened. Turn off the heat and place the bowl with the egg mixture over a bowl filled with iced water to cool.

Pour the cream into a large bowl and beat until thick, and soft peaks form. Fold the cooled egg mixture through the cream until thoroughly incorporated. Fold in the candied fruit and pour into a clean bowl. Cover with plastic wrap/clingfilm and freeze until firm.

Scoop and serve with cookies.

COOKS' NOTE: You can also line a loaf pan with plastic wrap/clingfilm and pour in the semifreddo. Once frozen invert the pan onto a serving plate and unmold. Cut into 1½-inch (4-cm) slices to serve.

3 US large/UK medium eggs

2 egg yolks

½ cup/100 g granulated/caster sugar

2 cups/500 ml heavy/double cream

3 tablespoons Candied Citrus (see page 116), finely chopped

cookies, to serve

an electric hand whisk

SERVES 6–8

Rioja & Allspice PEAR & BLACKBERRY GALETTE

1 lb./455 g ready-made puff pastry

4 cups/1.8 litre Rioja & Allspice Pears (see page 106)

1 3/4 cups/225 g fresh blackberries

1 egg, beaten

turbinado/demerara sugar, to dredge

a baking sheet lined with baking parchment

SERVES 6–8

This is a gorgeous dessert. The dark, moody colors of the pears and blackberries make it outstandingly beautiful and it is just so easy to make. Serve it warm with salted caramel ice cream—heaven.

Preheat the oven to 475°F (245°C) Gas 9.

Drain the pears into a bowl and reserve the rioja syrup. Cut the pears into thin wedges and set aside.

Pour the rioja syrup into a small pan and cook over a medium–high heat until it reduces and thickens. Remove from the heat and set aside.

Roll out the pastry on a lightly floured surface into a rectangle approximately 12-inches (30-cm) by 6-inches (15-cm) and place on the prepared baking sheet. Arrange the pear slices and blackberries on top leaving a 2-inch (5-cm) border all the way round. Fold the edges in and over the fruit, and brush the pastry with the beaten egg. Generously sprinkle with sugar.

Bake in the preheated oven for 15–20 minutes until brown and crusty. Serve warm with the rioja syrup poured over.

COOKS' NOTE: Vin Santo Plums and Spiced Apricots can be used instead of the Rioja & Allspice Pears.

LIQUEURS & CORDIALS

A lot of my friends have started making their own liqueurs and cordials, spurred on by the fact that they really are a breeze to make. A visit to the local farmers' market in the height of summer and you have all the goodies you could wish for. Plums are at their best in summer and there are bountiful varieties. Make a batch of wonderful Country Peach Schnapps (page 125) with perfect, summer, rosy peaches or Cherry Vodka (page 131) with dark, juicy red cherries. Best of all, liqueurs made ahead to be sipped in the dark winter months offer memories of a long hot summer.

When fall/autumn comes around pears, apples and quinces are in season and perfect time for the holidays and making Autumn Apple & Ginger Liqueur (page 124). Similar to pickling you can mix spices, herbs, and fruits into sensational elixirs. Drink them as they come or turn into wonderful cocktails to dazzle your guests.

Store them in pretty re-purposed bottles or great vintage finds. I collect beautiful second-hand glass decanters at thrift stores and when the holiday season arrives I pour my homemade liqueurs into them to serve at parties. It looks so pretty with the glass and beautifully colored liqueurs sparkling in candlelight. Offer them at the end of a meal as a digestif—a nice way to end a great evening with friends.

In the heat of summer when the sun is high there is nothing better than pulling out a pitcher/jug of icy cold cordial from the fridge and serving it in tall glasses over ice. Muddle fresh herbs in the glasses to add a refreshingly bright tang to the drinks.

There are a few childhood favorites that I have resurrected in this chapter like Scottish Barley Water (page 136). It was drunk with vigor all through my childhood summers. Old Fashioned Ginger Beer (page 132), another great favorite was used to make ice cream floats. Now it becomes part of a Dark & Stormy (page 132) to be lazily sipped when the weather gets hot.

Making these delightful drinks can be as easy as walking down a country lane and picking elderberry blossoms or foraging for wild berries and herbs. Use the freshest and ripest, local organic produce and, unlike pickling or bottling, you want the fruits to be very ripe and sweet.

Add candied peels and the syrups from spoon fruits to a bottle of vodka and let it infuse for 5 days. I like to keep these flavored vodkas in the freezer—they won't freeze because of the alcohol content—and then pour them over ice cream or sorbet. This is especially true of the Meyer Limoncello (page 124), which is a permanent fixture in my freezer.

There are no expensive tools of the trade needed to start brewing your own drinks. Always have a funnel that fits perfectly into bottles to hand for decanting. I use extra large glass jars with screw tops for steeping the fruits in alcohol, and always have a good amount of cheesecloth/muslin available for straining—you can of course use coffee filters instead if you prefer.

Homemade liqueurs and cordials make fantastic gifts so it is nice to take time and choose pretty labels. Handwritten ones add that personal touch or you can type them on a computer.

Meyer LIMONCELLO

12 Meyer lemons
3¼ cups/750 ml vodka

SYRUP

1 cup/200 g granulated/caster sugar
1½ cups/350 ml water

a large sterilized glass jar and sterilized bottles
  with airtight lids

MAKES 4½ CUPS (36 OZ.)/1 L

Limoncello is a wonderful Italian citrus liqueur. It is simple to make at home and especially when fragrant Meyer lemons, in all their floral glory, show up at the market.

Peel the lemon skin with a sharp vegetable peeler, avoiding the pith. Squeeze the juice from the lemons into a large sterilized glass jar and add the peel. Pour in the vodka and stir. Cover and set aside at room temperature for 2 weeks.

To make the syrup, bring the sugar and water to a boil in a saucepan over a medium–high heat. Reduce the heat and simmer for 10 minutes, stirring occasionally until the sugar has dissolved. Remove from the heat and allow to cool.

Add the syrup to the Limoncello mixture then set aside for 30 minutes. Strain the liqueur though a cheesecloth/muslin or coffee filter into a pitcher/jug. Decant into sterilized bottles and label. Store in the refrigerator or freezer for up to 12 months.

Autumn APPLE & GINGER LIQUEUR

peel of 8 apples
a 2-inch/5-cm piece fresh ginger, peeled
  and chopped
4 fresh bay leaves
4 cups/1 litre Knob Creek bourbon

SYRUP

½ cup/110 g light brown sugar
½ cup/125 ml water

sterilized glass bottles with airtight lids

MAKES 4½ CUPS (36 OZ.)/1 L

Apple season is in the fall/autumn and the cooler evenings always welcome a warming liqueur.

Place the apple peel, ginger, and bay leaves in the bottom of a large glass. Pour over the bourbon, cover, and set aside at room temperature for at least 3 weeks.

To make the syrup, bring the sugar and water to a boil in a saucepan over a medium–high heat. Reduce the heat and simmer for 8 minutes, stirring occasionally until the sugar has dissolved. Remove from the heat and allow to cool.

Add the syrup to the apple mixture then set aside for 30 minutes. Strain the liqueur though a cheesecloth/muslin or coffee filter into a pitcher/jug. Decant into sterilized bottles and label. Store in a cool, dark place for at least 2 months before serving.

Orange BITTERS

I love making orange bitters. It always look so pretty with curls of orange peel and spices in a large glass jar soaking in crystal-clear vodka.

Preheat the oven to 275°F (135°C) Gas 1.

Peel the orange skin with a sharp vegetable peeler, avoiding the pith. Place the peel on the prepared baking sheet and bake in the oven for 30 minutes or until dried and curled up. Remove from the oven and allow to cool.

Place the ginger, cardamom pods, star anise and cooled peel in a large sterilized glass jar and pour over the vodka. Cover and set aside at room temperature for 3 weeks.

To make the syrup, bring the sugar and water to a boil in a saucepan over a medium–high heat. Reduce the heat and simmer for 10 minutes, stirring occasionally until the sugar has dissolved. Remove from the heat and allow to cool.

Add the syrup to the bitters mixture let stand for 30 minutes then strain though a cheesecloth/muslin or coffee filter into a pitcher/jug. Decant into sterilized bottles and label. Store in a cool, dark place for at least 1 month before serving.

3 large oranges, peel reserved

2 teaspoons crystalized ginger

12 cardamom pods, bruised

4 whole star anise

2 fresh bay leaves

4 cups/1 litre vodka

SYRUP

2 cups/400 g granulated/caster sugar

1 cup/250 ml water

a baking sheet lined with baking parchment

a large sterilized glass jar and sterilized bottles with airtight lids

MAKES 4½ CUPS (36 OZ.)/1 L

Country PEACH SCHNAPPS

Juicy ripe peaches bathed in spices and vodka yield a wonderful aperitif just in time for the depth of winter.

Place the peach wedges, bay leaves, nutmeg, sugar, and vanilla in a large sterilized glass jar.

Pour the vodka over the peach mixture, cover, and set aside at room temperature for at least 1 month.

Strain the schnapps through a cheesecloth/muslin or coffee filter into a pitcher/jug, pushing down on the fruit to squeeze all the juices out. Decant into sterilized bottles and label. Store in the refrigerator or freezer for up to 12 months.

12 ripe peaches, stones removed and cut into wedges

4 fresh bay leaves

⅛ teaspoon ground nutmeg

¼ cup/55 g light brown sugar

1 vanilla bean/pod, halved and seeds removed

4 cups/1 litre vodka

a large sterilized glass jar and sterilized bottles with airtight lids

MAKES 4½ CUPS (36 OZ.)/1 L

Meyer LIMONCELLO CHAMPAGNE COCKTAIL

champagne, chilled, to top up
Meyer Limoncello (see page 124), chilled

6 champagne glasses, chilled
SERVES 6

Wonderful citrus Meyer Limoncello (see page 124)
meets bubbles—a fun, refreshing drink to kick off
cocktail hour. I really like to serve this at parties as it
is simple and fuss-free.

Pour a splash of Meyer Limoncello in the bottom of each chilled glass
and top with the champagne. Serve at once.

Connie's DELIGHT

I was having dinner with my friend Connie and the barman made this drink especially for her—a gorgeous amber color, almost too pretty to drink. She was delighted!

Rub the rims of chilled glasses with the orange peel, then drop them in the bottom of the glasses.

Fill a cocktail shaker with ice, pour in the bourbon, Noilly Pratt Rouge, Orange Bitters and a dash of angostura. Stir for 30 seconds. Do not shake. Strain into the chilled glasses, and serve.

crushed ice
4 orange peel twists
1 cup/250 ml Knob Creek bourbon
¼ cup/60 ml Noilly Pratt Rouge or other red vermouth
2 tablespoons Orange Bitters (see page 125)
a dash of angostura bitters

cocktail shaker and 4 glasses, chilled

SERVES 4

Cherry VODKA

Another great way to enjoy cherries. Cherry vodka can be used in cocktails, poured over sorbets or simply enjoy as an after-dinner digestif.

Prick each cherry a few times with a wooden skewer or toothpick/cocktail stick and place in a wide-mouthed sterilized glass jar.

Pour over the vodka and screw the lid on tightly. Store in a cool, dark place for at least 1 month before serving—the longer you leave the vodka the stronger the cherry flavor will become.

Decant into small bottles, seal and keep refrigerated for up to 12 months.

3 cups/455 g ripe cherries, rinsed
3 ¼ cups/750 ml vodka

a wide-mouthed sterilized glass jar with airtight lid
sterilized small bottles with airtight caps or flip lids
MAKES 4½ CUPS (36 OZ.)/1 L

Cherry VODKA MARTINI

Martinis are the most glamorous of all cocktails. They are timeless, wonderfully sophisticated, and for many people a wonderful way to finish the day.

Fill a cocktail shaker with crushed ice. Pour in the Cherry Vodka and vermouth and shake for 30 seconds.

Place a cherry or two in each glass and pour in the martini.

COOKS NOTE: If you want to serve the martinis on the rocks fill the glasses with crushed ice before pouring over the cocktail.

crushed ice
1 cup/250 ml Cherry Vodka (see above)
¼ cup/60 ml dry vermouth
cherries, to garnish

cocktail shaker and 4 glasses, chilled
SERVES 4

Old-fashioned GINGER BEER

2 x 4 1/2-in/11.5-cm piece of fresh ginger, peeled and finely chopped

1 1/4 cups/175 g superfine/caster sugar

grated zest and juice of 1 lemon

1 teaspoon active dry yeast

sterilized glass bottles with airtight caps or flip lids

MAKES 9 CUPS (72 OZ.)/2 L

My first attempt at making ginger beer was a disaster and all the bottles exploded. It didn't put me off. The key to avoid this is to screw the lids on loosely and keep checking throughout the 3-day fermentation that the ginger beer is not too fizzy, if it is, simply loosen the caps to release some of the bubbles.

Bring 5 cups/1.1 litres of water, the ginger and sugar to a boil in a saucepan over a medium–high heat. Reduce the heat and simmer for 10 minutes, stirring occasionally until the sugar has dissolved. Remove from the heat and cool until the liquid is just warm.

Add the lemon zest, juice, and the yeast. Stir, and cover with a lid. Set aside in a warm place for at least 24 hours.

Strain the ginger beer through a cheesecloth/muslin or coffee filter into sterilized into a pitcher/jug. Loosely screw the caps on and set aside in a cool, dark place for 3 days before serving. Store in the refrigerator for up to 4 days.

Dark & STORMY

crushed ice

1 cup/250 ml Goslings Black Seal rum or similar

Ginger Beer (see above), to top up

lime wedges, to serve

4 glasses, chilled

SERVES 4

Dark & Stormy is hailed as the national drink of Bermuda. Although its name sounds like trouble it is refreshing served over ice. Homemade ginger beer gives this drink a zestier flavor.

Fill the chilled glasses with crushed ice. Pour a 1/4 cup/60 ml of rum into each glass and top with Ginger Beer. Finish each glass with a squeeze of lime and serve.

Gingersnap CORDIAL

1½ teaspoons ground ginger
½ teaspoon ground cinnamon
½ teaspoon ground allspice
¼ teaspoon ground cloves
2 cups/400 g light brown sugar
4 cups/1 litre water
sparkling water, to top up
sterilized glass bottles with caps or flip lids
MAKES 7 CUPS (54 OZ.)/1.5 L

Spicy ginger cordial makes for a fantastic long drink in the hot summer months.

Place all the ingredients in a non-reactive pan and bring to a boil over a medium–high heat. Reduce the heat and simmer for 10 minutes, stirring occasionally until the sugar has dissolved. Remove from the heat, cover, and set aside to cool completely.

Strain the mixture through a cheesecloth/muslin or coffee filter into a pitcher/jug.

Serve over ice topped with sparkling water. Store in an airtight container in the refrigerator.

Lemongrass & Thyme CORDIAL

6 lemongrass stalks
1 small bunch of lemon thyme
peel of 1 lime
2 cups/400 g granulated/caster sugar
4 cups/1 litre water
sparkling water, to top up
sterilized glass bottles with caps or flip lids
MAKES 7 CUPS (54 OZ.)/1.5 L

Lemongrass exudes a wonderfully deep lemon and lime flavor. Marry that with lemon thyme and you have an earthy citrus mix. Use this cordial to make cocktails, and lemonades, as well as adding to iced teas.

Place all the ingredients in a non-reactive pan and bring to a boil over a medium–high heat. Reduce the heat and simmer for 10 minutes, stirring occasionally until the sugar has dissolved. Remove from the heat, cover, and set aside to cool completely.

Strain the mixture through a cheesecloth/muslin or coffee filter into a pitcher/jug, pushing the solids down to extract all the juices.

Serve over ice topped with sparkling water. Store in an airtight container in the refrigerator.

Damson PLUM LIQUEUR

Roasting the plums and herbs with a little sugar gives them a deep, intense, earthy flavor. The whole concoction creates a beautiful, dark-colored liqueur, which will make you smile.

Preheat the oven to 425°F (245°C) Gas 9.

Place the plums, thyme, rosemary, bay leaves, tarragon and brown sugar in a ceramic baking dish and mix. Roast in the preheated oven for 20 minutes or until the plums can be mashed.

Pour the mixture into a large sterilized glass jar and allow to cool—you don't need to remove the stones as it will be strained later. Pour over the vodka, cover, and set aside at room temperature for at least 3 weeks.

To make the syrup, bring the sugar and water to a boil in a saucepan over a medium–high heat. Reduce the heat and simmer for 8 minutes, stirring occasionally until the sugar has dissolved. Remove from the heat and allow to cool.

Strain the plum mixture through a cheesecloth/muslin or coffee filter into a pitcher/jug and stir in the cooled sugar syrup. Decant into sterilized bottles, seal and label. Store in a cool, dark place for at least 1 month before serving.

16 plums
2 teaspoons dried thyme
2 teaspoons fresh rosemary leaves
4 fresh bay leaves
4 tarragon sprigs
1/4 cup/55 g light brown sugar
4 cups/1 litre vodka

SYRUP

1 cup/200 g granulated/caster sugar
1/2 cup/125 ml water

a large sterilized glass jar and sterilized glass bottles with caps or flip lids

MAKES 4½ CUPS (36 OZ.)/1 L

Sour PLUM LIQUEUR

Sour plums are in season in the early stages of summer. If you can't find them at your farmers' market try Asian stores or supermarkets.

Layer the plums and rock sugar in a large sterilized glass jar, then pour in the vodka or soju. Cover, and place in a cool, dark place for at least 6 months.

Serve chilled in small sake glasses.

COOKS' NOTE: Soju is a Korean distilled liquid made from rice that is comparable to vodka. It is available online or at most Asian stores.

16 green sour plums, rinsed and stems removed
1 cup plus 2 tablespoons/225 g rock sugar/sugar crystals
4 cups/1 litre vodka or soju

a large sterilized glass jar and sterilized glass bottles with caps or flip lids

MAKES 4½ CUPS (36 OZ.)/1 L

Scottish BARLEY WATER

1 cup/185 g pearl barley, rinsed
8 cups/2 litres water
¼ cup/50 g superfine/caster sugar
grated zest and juice of 2 lemons

sterilized glass bottles with caps or flip lids
MAKES 9 CUPS (72 OZ.)/2 L

Every summer during the school holidays I made barley water—a drink from my childhood. It is supposed to be good for your complexion, another reason for drinking it apart from its great taste.

Place the barley in a large pan and add the water. Bring to a boil, then reduce the heat and simmer for 1 hour.

Strain the barley water into a large bowl, saving the barley for another use if desired. Stir the sugar into the hot liquid and set aside to cool. Once cooled, add the lemon juice and zest, pour into a large pitcher/jug or glass bottles and store in the refrigerator.

COOKS' NOTE: Use the reserved barley for soups and stews or in a barley salad with roasted vegetables.

Scottish BARLEY WATER
SLUSHES

crushed ice
Scottish Barley Water (see above)
sparkling water

TO SERVE

lemon wedges
mint

4 glasses, chilled
SERVES 4

Scottish Barley Water (see above) is a refreshing thirst-quencher. Bottle it, and take to the beach, or on a country picnic. Or even turn it into a cocktail with a splash of vodka when the sun goes down.

Fill the chilled glasses with crushed ice. Pour the Scottish Barley Water three-quarters of the way up the glasses, then top with sparkling water.

Drop a lemon wedge and sprig of mint into each glass, and serve.

Wild Blueberry CORDIAL

Wild blueberries are smaller than the ones that you find in your local store. If you are lucky and live in an area where they grow then harvest as many as you can. If you can't find wild blueberries you can make this with store-bought ones.

Purée the blueberries, lemon juice and 1 cup (235 ml) of water in a food processor until smooth.

Bring the sugar and water to a boil in a saucepan over a medium–high heat. Reduce the heat and simmer for 10 minutes, stirring occasionally until the sugar has dissolved. Set aside to cool, then add to the blueberry purée.

Decant into sterilized bottles, seal and label. Store in the refrigerator for up to 12 months.

3½ cups/455 g wild blueberries
3 tablespoons freshly squeezed lemon juice

SYRUP
1½ cups/275 g superfine/caster sugar
1½ cups/675 ml water

sterilized glass bottles with caps or flip lids

MAKES 4½ CUPS (36 OZ.)/1 L

Wild Blueberry
SUMMER COOLERS

I first made this on visit to Maine where blueberries grow wild along the edge of the road. We had a glut of blueberries so it seemed the next logical step was making a refreshing drink.

Fill the chilled glasses with crushed ice. Pour the Wild Blueberry Cordial half of the way up the glasses and top up with sparkling water.

Garnish with mint, and serve.

COOKS NOTE: Serve the coolers in sterilized soda bottles for a picnic or outdoor dining.

crushed ice
Wild Blueberry Cordial (see above)
sparkling water, to top up
mint, to garnish (optional)

4 glasses or sterilized soda bottles, chilled

SERVES 4

Elderberry CORDIAL

Once a year, at my local market, a Swedish farmer turns up with elderflowers. It is such a beautiful sight of frilly white blossoms announcing that summer is here. You wouldn't believe that such beauty can also make amazing drinks as well as producing a exotic cargo of berries which then become preserves.

Place the sugar in a large bowl and pour over the boiling water. Stir until the sugar is dissolved. Add the rinsed elderflower and stir to mix. Cover and set aside to cool overnight.

Strain the mixture through a cheesecloth/muslin or coffee filter into a pitcher/jug. Store in an airtight container in the refrigerator for up to 12 months.

2¼ cups/450 g of white sugar
2 cups/500 ml boiling water
12 elderflower heads, rinsed

MAKES 3 CUPS (24 OZ.)/700 ML

Elderberry SNOW CONES

finely crushed ice
1 cup/250 ml vodka
Elderberry Cordial (see above), to top up
elderberries or blossoms ,to garnish (optional)

4 glasses, chilled
SERVES 4

These are grown-up snow cones laced with vodka. Almost too pretty to drink, the ice is crushed so finely it looks like snow. Dress them up with a pretty garnish of elderberries or blossom.

Fill the chilled glasses with crushed ice, then pour a ¼ cup/60 ml of vodka into each glass. Top with Elderberry Cordial.

Garnish each glass with elderberries or blossom and serve.

INDEX

ACKNOWLEDGMENTS

The team got together again this summer in my kitchen to cook and shoot. Huge thanks to my friends, Erin Kunkel for her stunningly beautiful photography and to Sandra Tripicchio's culinary skills and tireless work alongside me. As always it was a lot of fun. Jennifer Barguiarena for her pretty props. E. A. Alvarino Antiques, Scotland, for the gorgeous antique flatware. Thank you to Julia Charles, Leslie Harrington and Stephanie Milner for making it all possible. Geoff Borin for his wonderful design. My husband for tasting everything with a smile. It couldn't have been possible without all of you. Thank you!